# THE HIGH ANDES

## A GUIDE FOR CLIMBERS

### John Biggar

Published by Andes, 1996

**ISBN  1-871890-38-1**


**PUBLISHER**
Published in 1996 by Andes, 93 Queen Street, Castle Douglas, Kirkcudbrightshire, DG7 1EH, SCOTLAND. Phone/Fax 01556 503929

**DISCLAIMER**
Mountaineering is an inherently dangerous activity. The author accepts no liability whatsoever for any loss, injury or inconvenience resulting from the use of this guide.

Printed by Joseph Ward Colour Print Ltd, The Ring Road, Dewsbury, WF13 1HR.
Trade distribution by Cordee, 3a DeMontfort Street, Leicester, LE1 7HD, GREAT BRITAIN.

Front cover photograph:  **Jatunhuma seen from the normal route on Campa, Cordillera Vilcanota, Peru**. J. Biggar
Opposite: **North face of Huascaran Norte from the normal route on Pisco Oeste, Cordillera Blanca, Peru**. J. Biggar

# CONTENTS

# MAIN MAPS

Simon Bolivar
MERIDA  CARACAS
COLOMBIA  Bolivar  VENEZUELA
S.N. del Cocuy
Los Nevados  BOGOTÁ
ECUADOR  QUITO  equator
Chimborazo  MANAOS
PERU  BRAZIL
Cord. Blanca
Huascaran
HUARAZ  Yerupajá
Cord. Huayhuash  LIMA  CUZCO  BOLIVIA
Cord. Vilcanota
Cord. Real
AREQUIPA  LA PAZ
Sajama
ARICA
Cord. Occidental
SAO PAULO
CALAMA  RIO DE JANEIRO
Llullaillaco  SALTA
Puna de Atacama
Incahuasi
COPIAPO  Ojos del Salado
Pissis  Bonete
CATAMARCA
Mercedario
High Andes  Aconcagua
SANTIAGO  MENDOZA
Tupungato
CHILE  BUENOS AIRES

**Map 1**

| 0 | 500 | 1000 | 1500km |

ARGENTINA

**THE ANDES**

Showing principal mountain ranges,
the ten highest peaks, and the
highest peaks in each country.
Important access cities in CAPITALS

Torres del Paine

# INTRODUCTION

The Andes are one of the world's greatest mountain ranges, second in height to only the Himalayas. The range extends the full length of the west coast of South America, often rising straight from the Pacific. Much of the range consists of an upland plateau from 3000-4500m high from which isolated mountain ranges rise known as 'Cordilleras' or 'Nudos'.

The Andes offer mountaineers an experience that is in many ways half way between the European Alps and the Himalayas. In terms of height, difficulty and access the Andes fall somewhere between the relatively civilised mountains of Europe or North America and the wild peaks of Asia. They are an ideal destination for experienced mountaineers aspiring to greater heights or remoter peaks without the bureaucratic problems of a Himalayan expedition.

Within the Andes one can choose from a complete range of mountaineering experiences. There is something for everyone, from easily ascended volcanoes to desperate ice faces. Peru and Bolivia are countries still steeped in the culture of the Incas, but Chile and Argentina are modern nations very much like a part of Europe. The Andes of Venezuela and Ecuador rise from tropical forests, those of northern Chile rise above the driest desert in the world.

## SCOPE OF THIS GUIDE

This guide covers only the high peaks of the Andes, including all 6000m peaks and the most accessible and popular 5000m peaks, which are found from Venezuela in the north to as far south as Santiago in Chile. The mountains of Patagonia are not included.

This guide is intended for the average mountaineer on a first or second visit to the Andes who wants to climb some big peaks by moderately interesting routes. In most cases only the easiest ascent of any peak is described in detail, with other harder routes being mentioned where they are climbed relatively often. The most technically difficult routes are not detailed.

The guide assumes a basic ability to route find in Alpine terrain and as a consequence fairly brief descriptions are given.

Information is as reliable and accurate as possible but because this guide is a compilation from many sources complete reliability cannot be guaranteed. Personal experience or the knowledge of friends was used for many of the routes described. Other reliable sources (such as Spanish language guidebooks) have been used for many other routes. However to produce a comprehensive guide some peaks have been included for which information is scanty. Hopefully this will inspire further exploration.

This guide is intended to be used along with a good general travel guide to the countries concerned which will provide more general information about transport, hotels, etc.

# USING THIS GUIDE

The mountains of the Andes are described from North to South, split as logically as possible into ranges and areas. Where necessary a West to East order has been used. There is an introduction for each area detailing general conditions. Base towns and cities are described at the start of each section or sub-section.

## TIMES
Timings given in the heading bars are for a return trip to climb one peak approaching from the base town listed in the access section. Climbing several summits in one area will obviously save on approach times. All times assume climbers are already acclimatised to the height of the normal base camp and are reasonably fit. Times assume no delays in travelling to the mountain and as little walking as possible. They allow for no route finding problems and no spare days for bad weather, but do allow for further days of acclimatisation high on the mountains if these are thought to be necessary for the average climber. To be sure of a successful ascent it would be wise to plan an extra day or more to allow for unforeseen circumstances.

## GRADES
Standard UIAA alpine grades (F, PD, AD, D, TD, ED ) are given for the easiest ascent route in 'normal' conditions. These should be found consistent in any one range but because of the variety of sources used there may be some variation between ranges. Split grades denote either some uncertainty or mountains where conditions are very variable. N/K or n/k denotes grade unknown - an estimated idea of the difficulty will usually be found in the text. Pitch grades are occasionally given using the standard UIAA system (I, II, III, IV for rock and 50° etc. for snow or ice). A rough comparison table for rock grades follows.

| UIAA | British | American |
|------|---------|----------|
| I | Mod | 5.2 |
| II | Diff | 5.3 |
| III | V. Diff | 5.4 |
| IV | 4a-4b | 5.5-5.6 |
| V | 4b-4c | 5.6-5.7 |

## NAMES
Names and heights used in the descriptions are normally those on the recommended Best Map. Alternatives are given if they are in common use. Translations are given where these are available but many mountain names are not translatable.

## MAPS AND DIAGRAMS
Maps are intended to help with orientation only and are of very limited use for navigation. A 'road' may only be passable to high wheel base 4WD, a walking route does not imply there is a path and a campsite sign does not imply there is any water. Refer to the text for more specific information. Where necessary railways are indicated by a single line with cross hatching. All maps face north unless indicated.

In areas where most routes are on easy volcanoes normally only a map is given. In areas where climbs are more technical diagrams are used more extensively. Diagrams have been drawn with their features stylised as per the key diagram. See page 155 for a key map, key diagram and list of abbreviations used.

# GENERAL ADVICE FOR  TRAVEL TO THE ANDES

### VISAS
At present visas are not needed by most US, Canadian and EC citizens for short stays (up to 60-90 days) in any of the Andean nations. French, Spanish and Portuguese citizens need visas for some countries and Australian, New Zealand and South African citizens will need visas for most countries. Other nationalities may need visas for some or all of the countries. The requirements are sure to change so it is best to check with the embassy in your country.

### FLYING TO SOUTH AMERICA
From Europe and the UK there are three main options. **1.** Fly with a European airline via a European capital e.g. Air France via Paris, KLM via Amsterdam, Iberia via Madrid or Lufthansa via Frankfurt. This is often the best option in terms of service and economy, but flights may only be once or twice a week. **2.** Fly with either United or American Airlines via Miami in the USA. This is usually a bit more expensive but the service is very good and there are daily schedules to almost all big South American cities. **3.** Fly with a South American airline, either direct or via some other South American city - these flights are usually cheaper but the service (with the exception of Varig) is not very good or reliable. However, you may get a very good deal with a South American airline if you also need an internal flight in the country concerned. London is served only by Varig (Brazil), Aerolineas Argentinas and VIASA (Venezuela). In Europe the cities of Madrid, Paris, Milan and Frankfurt are well served by LAN-Chile, Aerolineas Argentinas, Varig, VIASA and Avianca (of Colombia).
From North America the best option is almost always to fly via Miami which is served daily by all the major national South American airlines. United and American Airlines also have daily services from Miami to most South American cities. The South American airlines are cheaper but United and American have much better service. There are also some direct flights from Los Angeles, New York and Toronto.
From Australasia there are LAN-Chile (via NZ) and Aerolineas Argentinas (from Sydney) flights direct across the Pacific or flights, often on US airlines, via Los Angeles and/or Miami.
Further details of how to get to each area of the Andes are given in the text.

### BUDGET AND MONEY
South America is not particularly cheap. Mostly it is not expensive either, but expect to pay prices similar to those in the US or Europe for most services, particularly in the more expensive countries like Chile and Argentina. Public transport everywhere is usually a bargain. If you need to save money you can use budget hotels and eat from street stalls, but on an expedition with specific mountaineering objectives these measures may be counterproductive if you end up ill or have all your equipment stolen.

An average expedition staying in clean and secure hotels, eating in reasonable restaurants and using some hired transport and mule services will work out at about $30 per person per day, noticeably more for ascents of Aconcagua or very remote Puna mountains, slightly less in Ecuador and Bolivia. Budgeting carefully and always using public transport you could easily half this figure and still have a great time.

Money should be taken in a mixture of US$ cash, US$ travellers cheques and credit cards (AMEX, VISA, MasterCard). Cash dollars can be used readily in most countries and may get you a discount. They can always be used if you're stuck for local currency. Travellers cheques can be changed fairly easily in all the main cities in this guide. Credit cards are accepted widely by larger businesses in all cities.

## SPANISH

The more Spanish you speak the easier your trip to South America will be. Some knowledge is **essential**. Only in Cuzco and a few other tourist centres is much English spoken. Out in the mountains there is **no chance** of finding anyone who speaks English. It is a fact that people with poor Spanish are more likely to be taken advantage of by muleteers, jeep drivers etc. You have to be able to negotiate and make yourself understood to get good prices and good service.

## ACCOMMODATION

This guide does not list recommended hotels for which a regular travel guide will be useful. Hotel accommodation varies enormously in price and you don't always get what you pay for, particularly when you start paying more. In most cities in this book you'll get a comfortable bed, with private bathroom for about $15-$20 for two sharing. Accommodation down to about $10 per pair can still be very reasonable, but budget accommodation tends to be just that - shabby, insecure and with poor service. Camping is not a practical option in South American cities.

## SECURITY

The author has lost only one pair of old running shoes in 8 years of travelling in South America. You don't have to be paranoid about rip-offs, just sensible. Don't get drunk, wander into poor parts of town, walk down quiet alleys or walk by yourself at night. If you do any of these you may get ripped off - if you do more than one you are almost sure to be ripped off.

Be especially careful in markets and at bus stations and anywhere that there are lots of tourists. Take taxis round town if arriving late or leaving early or if you've lots of luggage. Never put a bag down in the street. Keep your camera hidden.

Armed robbery and banditry, often linked to the drug trade, does occur occasionally but is extremely rare in Chile and Argentina. This is not a problem that should stop anyone going to South America but always take local advice about the current situation.

## ACCLIMATISATION AND ALTITUDE

Anyone travelling to the Andes must make themselves aware of the symptoms of altitude sickness, both mild and severe. Read and absorb a good textbook such as 'Medical Handbook for Mountaineers' by Steele, or better still read one specifically on Altitude Illness such as 'Altitude Illness' by Bezruchka. Generally speaking at least a week should be spent over 4000m before contemplating an ascent to over 6000m. Many towns and base camp areas are around this height in the Andes. While your body gets used to the altitude you can climb lower peaks, trek, or enjoy the cultural and archaeological sites that are numerous in the Andean nations.

Fitness, particularly heart and lung fitness, certainly improves acclimatisation. However, fit people may be more susceptible to altitude illness because they can do so much more. Experience suggests that the best method to avoid problems is to be fit before arrival then 'underexercise' i.e. do considerably less than you would on an equivalent trip to the Alps or Rockies. This means some sitting around so bring a good book, a pack of cards, or a pair of binoculars.

## HEALTH
For most of the countries concerned the following immunisations are advisable: Tetanus, Typhoid, Polio and Hepatitis. The vaccine for Cholera is generally not very effective. Yellow fever and Malaria precautions are only needed if you will be below 2500m in forest areas i.e. Venezuela, Colombia, Ecuador and the Amazon side of the Andes in Peru and Bolivia.
Biting insects are very rare in the mountains, but dogs can be a nuisance - throw a stone or pretend to throw a stone - some dogs will even back off if you pretend to pick up a stone!
A basic medical kit should be carried with plasters, blister kit, needle and thread, spare lip salve, scissors, strong safety pins and some pills for diarrhoea, headaches, coughs, purifying water and perhaps altitude sickness. On more remote trips consider anti-biotics (but don't use them for diarrhoea!), anti-histamine, strong painkillers, eyedrops and an anti-inflammatory. Carry some bits and pieces for general repairs to non-body parts, e.g. string, wire, strong tape and superglue.

# PLANNING A MOUNTAINEERING EXPEDITION

## PEAK FEES
At the time of going to press there were no peak fees as such for any of the mountains in this guide but the threat of governments deciding to impose them is increasing. There are peak fees for some mountains in Chilean Patagonia and there is a hefty national park fee of $80 for foreigners to climb Aconcagua (but they do keep the mountain very clean!).

## MAPS
Alpenvereinskarte of Austria publish a few maps of the Cordillera Blanca and Cordillera Real. Otherwise the best maps are generally those published by the Instituto Geografico Militar (IGM) of the country concerned. These are usually only available from the head office in the capital city. Though they will be found useful, these maps are generally poor. Rivers, roads and snowfields are often incorrectly marked and such features should not be relied on.
The best general large scale maps of the Andes are the ITMB Publishing 1:4,000,000 series, sheets 081 and 155. (Fax ITMB in Canada - 604 687 5925) In the UK it's worth trying The Map Shop (01684 593146) or Stanford's (0171 836 1321) to obtain these and other larger scale maps. Either shop may occasionally have a few IGM maps in stock if you're lucky!
The addresses for the national IGM's are as follows. Opening hours vary - it is best to go in the morning.

| | |
|---|---|
| Venezuela | Edificio Camejo, 1st Floor, Avenida Este 6, (south side) |
| Colombia | Agustin Codazzi, Carrera 30 # 48-51, Bogota |
| Ecuador | On hill, Av. T. Paz y Miño, off Av. Colombia, Quito |
| Peru | Av. Aramburu 1190, San Isidro, Lima (best to take a taxi) |

| Bolivia | Edificio Murillo, Calle Murillo, La Paz. The entrance is round the back in an alley off Calle Diagonal. |
| Chile | Dieciocho 369, Santiago (Metro station Los Heroes) |
| Argentina | Cabildo 301, Casilla 1426, (Subte D to Ministero Carranza), Buenos Aires |

## OTHER GUIDEBOOKS

As already stated, this guide does not include general travel information which can be obtained in many other guidebooks. Particularly recommended are the South American Handbook and the Lonely Planet guides. Other climbing and walking guides which might be useful are mentioned in each area introduction - these may not be in print but you may be lucky to find a copy somewhere. 'Mountaineering in the Andes' by Jill Neate is a very useful book for tracking down journal references to obscure peaks and routes.

## PUBLIC TRANSPORT

Most peaks in this guide can be reached reasonably well using public transport. Exceptions are mainly in the Cordillera Occidental of Chile and Bolivia, the Puna de Atacama as well as some of the more remote Peruvian and Bolivian ranges. Good areas to go to if you'll only be using public transport are Ecuador, Cordillera Blanca, parts of the Cordillera Real, the Sajama area of the Cord. Occidental and the Mendoza and Santiago area. Even in these areas a short and cheap taxi ride will often save a long walk.

The abbreviation (PT) in the text denotes the last place on the way to a mountain which can be reached easily and regularly using public transport. Specific details of transport connections are not given as they change so frequently and are available in general travel guides.

## HIRED TRANSPORT

In many areas the best way to reach the mountain is by hiring a jeep or similar vehicle with driver. This is relatively expensive but very convenient. Expect to pay about $100 for a drop-off 100km away (and another $100 to get picked up). Some spoken Spanish and prior knowledge of your road are very useful to help negotiate a good price. With a brief written contract and a written record of collection dates and times most drivers are very reliable. To find a driver in an unfamiliar town try either tourist agencies, car hire companies or mountaineering organisations - see individual entries. For short journeys on good roads just use taxi drivers.

## MOUNTAIN RESCUE

Rely only on your own skill, judgement and preparation.

With the exception of Aconcagua there is little organised mountain rescue in South America and on most of the higher peaks rescue is extremely unlikely if not impossible. Expeditions should be self sufficient and able to effect their own rescue. In a few areas where mountaineering is better developed e.g. Cordillera Blanca, Cordillera Real, Ecuador, there is an informal system in place where the local 'guides' will assist any mountaineers in trouble but this is **likely to take several days** at least.

## DONKEYS AND MULES

In many parts of the Andes donkeys, mules or horses are available to assist with establishing a base camp. They will always come with an arriero (horseman) to look after them. Their services can be unreliable and if at all possible it is better to rely on them just for casual assistance - i.e.

pack a rucksack you could carry if you had to, then get a donkey to do the hard work. Many expeditions have been stranded by having more than they could carry when the donkeys didn't turn up. Where their use is unavoidable, such as for approaching more technical or remote peaks, be sure that you can speak Spanish to the arriero. Try to get a written contract (though he may not be able to write). Going through an agency in a town or city will put up the price but eliminate some of the hassles.

Donkeys can carry 40kg, mules and horses up to 60kg. Prices are extremely variable. Normal rates in Peru and Bolivia are about $4 per day per animal and $8 per day per arriero, but on Aconcagua expect to pay $50 or more per animal per day. In Peru and Bolivia you will be expected to feed and shelter your arriero, or at least pay for his food.

## PORTERS

Porters are available in only a few parts of the Andes, such as on the busier peaks of Peru and Bolivia. In many places either the standard of living is too high for this to be attractive work or there is not the mountaineering infrastructure to support these jobs. Rates are about $6 per man per day.

Do not use children - giving a 15kg sack to a 12 year old boy or girl to carry is child abuse, and no civilised person should attempt to justify it as fair labour.

## GUIDES

There are mountain guides available in a few of the main mountaineering centres in South America. They almost never have the same level of training and experience as a European or North American guide, even the UIAGM approved guides in Peru. Their limited equipment may be of dubious quality. However, guides will almost always have very good knowledge of the local mountains and conditions, be good at organising arrieros, porters etc. and be very fit at altitude. For these reasons they can be well worth hiring.

## CAMPING FOOD

Most cities have a reasonably good supermarket somewhere - see individual entries. The quality and variety of food is very good in Chile and Argentina though some dried food should perhaps be brought from home. Supermarkets are less good in Peru, Ecuador and Bolivia, except in the bigger cities. They are often harder to find, tucked away in an affluent suburb. For these countries it's a good idea to bring more dried food from home. In smaller cities, notably Huaraz, there are no good supermarkets though most supplies can be hunted down eventually.

Useful camping food always available in South America includes :- staples such as bread, flour, sugar, dried milk, tea and coffee, packet soups, porridge oats, dried potato mix and pasta. Also available are chocolate bars and tasty biscuits (not cheap), boiled sweets, powdered fruit drinks.

Items not usually available include :- freeze dried food, dehydrated meals, good quality dried fruit and nuts, instant puddings.

In some areas such as Huaraz, Cuzco and La Paz, cooks can be employed for your camp.

## FUEL

The recommended fuel to use in South America has to be paraffin (referred to throughout this guide by the more universal name kerosene) because it is cheap and easily available from almost all petrol (automobile gas) stations and burns more cleanly and safely than petrol. Petrol can cause many problems with clogged stoves, white gas (Coleman fuel) is hard to get hold of in many places and methylated spirits is difficult to find and totally impractical due to the large quantities needed. The best alternative to a kerosene based stove is a camping gas stove, but the cylinders are expensive, can be hard to find and you can't take them on an aeroplane.

## RENTING AND BUYING EQUIPMENT IN SOUTH AMERICA

If you can possibly avoid it do so. There is some equipment for purchase and rental and in major centres like Huaraz, Cuzco and La Paz you may even get half decent equipment, but the choice is usually very limited and climbing equipment is of dubious origin. In many areas finding any equipment will be a long job.

# CLIMBING CONDITIONS AND HAZARDS

Only conditions and hazards particular to the Andes are mentioned here. All areas suffer to some extent from the usual mountain hazards of bad weather, loose rock, avalanches etc.

## SUN

The sun is much stronger in the Andes than in Europe and the USA. It is higher in the sky, the air is thinner, there are fewer clouds and there is generally more snow cover. A hat with brim and neck flap, glacier goggles and high factor sun cream and lip salve are essential for a safe expedition.

## GLACIERS

True valley glaciers are not common in the High Andes, with glaciers normally only found on the steeper upper parts of mountains. The main exceptions are the Cordillera Vilcanota in Peru, where there are also a few large ice-caps, and the Santiago area where glaciers flow down some of the valleys. The Glacier Juncal Sur (15km) may be the longest glacier in the area covered by this guide. No glacier in the Cordillera Blanca is even 5km long. (There are of course some enormous 100km long glaciers in the Patagonian Andes.) Glaciers are receding everywhere.
Seracs and crevasses on glaciers should be treated with the same caution as anywhere. In the tropical areas crevasses tend to be larger than they are in the temperate Alps or Rockies.

## SNOW AND ICE

Snow and ice tend to be very stable in the Andes in the climbing seasons. Long spells without precipitation, very cold nights and strong sun probably account for this. Avalanches undoubtedly happen but seem to be relatively rare in  the climbing seasons. Ecuador with its stormier climate has the worst reputation and Colombia is probably bad too.
In the tropical areas, from Colombia to Bolivia, all but the steepest parts of the mountains are glaciated. Steep serac covered slopes are a feature of this area and make the mountains look very different to the bare rock faces of the summertime Alps or Rockies. In some parts of the Andes snow lies on faces up to 70° and forms unconsolidated snow flutings which give rise to very precarious climbing. The Peruvian Cordilleras (Blanca, Huayhuash, Vilcabamba and Vilcanota) are particularly notorious for these beautiful but dangerous features. In much of Peru there is generally good quality hard ice on north facing slopes while the shaded south facing slopes have the worst of the unconsolidated powder snow. East and west slopes are a bit of a mixture.

Further south, the Cordillera Real of Bolivia has very stable conditions and some of the best hard snow and ice on all faces during the very cold months of June and July. In the Puna and Cordillera Occidental the small glaciers and snowfields also remain hard all day. Avalanches are very rare in these areas.

Conditions around Mendoza and Santiago tend to be more like the Alps or Rockies in summer, with snow softening considerably during the day and freezing again overnight. Snow does not lie on such steep faces, so there are generally more exposed rock faces in this part of the Andes.

## PENITENTES

Penitentes are vertical spikes of snow or ice common throughout the Andes. At 20cm they are a mild nuisance but at 5m they can make a climb virtually impossible. Formed due to accumulations of dust they are at their worst in the driest areas such as the Puna de Atacama and Cordillera Occidental, but are common also around Aconcagua and in parts of Peru and Bolivia. They tend to line up in rows and going with the grain is much easier than going across it. Penitentes can often be seen with binoculars or a sharp eye and avoided. In the Santiago-Mendoza area they grow during the summer and will be at their worst in February.

On the good side penitentes are responsible for the lower avalanche risk in parts of the Andes.

## ROCK QUALITY

There are few areas of the Andes renowned for good quality rock. Volcanic areas such as the Puna, Cord. Occidental and Ecuador tend to have extremely poor rock. Much of the Cord. Blanca, Cord. Real and the High Andes of Chile and Argentina are composed of poor shale type rock, though in all three regions there are areas of granite which give better climbing.

## MINEFIELDS

These are signalled in Spanish by 'Zona de minas' or 'Campo de minas' and/or 'Peligro'. They are a hazard in passes on or near the Chile-Bolivia and Chile-Argentina borders. Attempts to find out whether these are anti-vehicle mines or anti-personnel mines have not been successful and it should be presumed they are dangerous. Though usually fenced the mine fields are not always well marked (and certainly not on maps) and it is possible to come across a sign only when leaving an area! Any fence, upright or not, in a remote border area should be treated with suspicion.

## LACK OF WATER

On many peaks in the Cordillera Occidental and Puna de Atacama lack of water is a serious hazard. The following notes give some tactics for dealing with this logistical problem but the seriousness of running out of water in a remote desert mountain should never be underestimated. Allow at least 5 litres per day per person and don't put all your supply in one big water barrel!

Snow can fall at any time of year (a bit more often in the winter months of JJAS) and will lie for some weeks. A recent snowfall will make water logistics much easier. In some cases an acclimatised party can reach the snow line in only one day from the nearest road. In other situations water can be ferried uphill separately from the other equipment. The dry climate and easy nature of the mountains mean a lightweight bivvy expedition can help offset having to carry water. Another tactic is to climb higher and carry snow back down to a lower camp - this is easier than carrying water up hill but should only be attempted if easily achievable.

# EQUIPMENT

### CAMPING EQUIPMENT

Tents used at altitude need to be lightweight and strong to survive the occasional storm force winds. There are many such tents available these days e.g. North Face MTN24 and VE25 or Terra Nova Quasar and Hyperspace. Stoves should be robust, able to melt snow quickly and easy to repair in the field. The MSR XGK-II is able to burn almost any petroleum product (but best with white gas or kerosene) and is in a class of its own, though other manufacturers are bringing out similar stoves now. At altitude a cigarette lighter may be easier to use than matches - flames don't burn well without oxygen!

Very low temperatures (-20ºC) at night mean a 5 season sleeping bag is more or less essential for camps above 5500m, particularly in southern Peru, Bolivia and the Puna in the coldest months of June and July.

### MOUNTAINEERING EQUIPMENT

An ice-axe and crampons are needed for almost every ascent in this guide. The majority of routes are also on glaciers and full precautions against a crevasse fall must be taken. This will require a rope, harnesses, prussik loops and snow and ice belay equipment - and, of course, the knowledge of how to use this equipment to prevent a serious crevasse fall is also crucial. An improvised chest harness should be used especially when carrying a heavy rucksack.

Harder routes will obviously require a second ice tool and more belay equipment. Snow stakes and ice-screws are the most commonly used items on the harder routes in Peru and Bolivia, with rock protection obviously useful on the few mixed routes.

Ski poles are strongly recommended because they save energy, on loose ground (like snow or scree) and are particularly useful at altitude and when carrying heavy packs. As most of the Andean peaks will involve all three factors at the same time, two poles should be carried. Energy savings of c.20-30% easily make them worth the extra weight.

### CLOTHING

In most areas clothing suitable for a summer trip to the European Alps will be suitable for climbing most 6000m peaks. It can feel extremely hot on a glacier at 6000m in the sunshine, but in bad weather hypothermia and frostbite are very real dangers. A modern flexible clothing system should be used. Essential items for all peaks are several fleece layers and a complete windproof shell, a warm hat and mountain gloves.

Temperatures at night drop a lot lower than they do in the Alps so a very good sleeping bag should be used. An extra layer of clothes for cold early morning starts will also be useful. Wind chill is an added hazard particularly in the Puna de Atacama and on Aconcagua.

### NAVIGATION

An altimeter is a highly recommended piece of navigation equipment for many peaks in this guide. None of the published maps are adequate, especially for navigation in bad weather or at night. In order to safely retrace your steps from a summit an altimeter can be used to complement your compass, since pacing and timing do not work at altitude and on loose or steep ground. A written note of altitudes, reference points and bearings taken on the way up should get you back down in poor conditions.

# WHERE TO GO AND WHEN TO CLIMB

Two main factors determine climbing seasons in South America. South of the Tropic of Capricorn (Mendoza-Santiago area and to a lesser extent the Puna) the best time to climb is the southern hemisphere summer. In the tropical areas covering the remainder of the Andes the best time to climb is the dry season which is in winter for the area concerned - i.e. in July for Peru and Bolivia and in January for Colombia and Venezuela. There are two transition zones with less well defined seasons - Ecuador is wet most of the year and the Atacama area is dry all year.

The other two main considerations are whether you wish to climb easier volcanic peaks or harder 'alpine' peaks (see table), and what sort of cultural experience you want. If you want to see llamas, traditional costumes and bustling markets then go to either Peru, Bolivia or Ecuador. If you want a modern country and infrastructure with big air conditioned buses and supermarkets go to Chile or Argentina. Venezuela and Colombia are about half way between the two extremes. This advice should be treated only as a useful generalisation as all the Andean countries are a bit of a mixture between the old and the modern.

| AREA | GO | PEAKS | ACCESS |
|---|---|---|---|
| VENEZUELA | NDJFMA | 4500-5000m Alpine | Easy |
| COLOMBIA | DJFMA | 4500-5500m Alpine and Volcanic | Medium |
| ECUADOR | All Year ex MAM | 5000-6300m Volcanic | Easy |
| PERU - Cordillera Blanca | MJJAS | 5000-6700m Alpine | Easy |
| PERU - Cord. Huayhuash and Central | MJJAS | 5000-6500m Alpine | Medium |
| PERU - Cord. Vilcanota and Urubamba | MJJAS | 5000-6400m Alpine | Medium |
| PERU/BOLIVIA/CHILE - Cordillera Occidental | All Year | 5500-6700m Volcanic | Medium - Difficult |
| BOLIVIA - Cord. Real | MJJAS | 5000-6400m Alpine | Easy |
| ARGENTINA - Chañi and Cachi | MJJAS | 5500-6500m Alpine and Volcanic | Medium - Difficult |
| ARGENTINA/CHILE Puna de Atacama | All year ex MJJA | 5500-6900m Volcanic | Difficult |
| ARGENTINA/CHILE Mendoza to Santiago | DJFM | 5000-7000m Alpine and Volcanic | Easy - Medium |

# ENVIRONMENTAL IMPACT AND RESPONSIBLE TOURISM

There is no excuse for the poor attitude of previous generations and previous expeditions. People will follow in your footsteps and have to suffer the consequences of your actions.

1.   Travel as a small lightweight group. This is guaranteed to reduce your impact.
2.   Carry as little as possible into the mountains and all your rubbish back out.
3.   Be careful where you defecate. In busy areas try to go during the day when away from camps if at all possible, or walk a long way (downhill) from the camp. Do not foul water or snow supplies.
4.   Do not light any fires anywhere. Use only a camping stove for cooking.
5.   Never give unearned gifts. This only encourages begging. If you give a present in return for a favour or good service try to make it a useful or educational item e.g. a pen and paper for a child, a pocket knife for an arriero.
6.   Never give children sweets - they don't have dentists.
7.   Respect privacy when taking photos.

# UPDATES

Users of this guide should be aware that while the author has done everything to ensure it is as accurate as possible, it would be impossible for this guide to be completely up to date. Though every care has been taken in compiling this information, climbing routes (particularly those on glaciers) are subject to continual change and new roads are always opening up new possibilities for access.

All chapters will be updated as frequently as practical. If you wish to receive an updated version of any part of this guidebook please write or fax us at the address below for availability and prices.

Users are requested to send any updated or improved information on climbing routes, access etc. to the publisher so that we can improve future editions of this guide. All major contributions will receive a free copy of the next edition. Please send any information to:

Andes, 93 Queen Street, Castle Douglas, DG7 1EH, SCOTLAND.
Phone/Fax 00 44 1556 503929

Further copies of this guide can be obtained from this address by mail order if you have trouble finding it in your local shops.

# THE AUTHOR

John Biggar has been climbing in the Andes regularly for the past eight years. When not in South America he lives in Castle Douglas where he runs 'Andes' a business specialising in trekking and mountaineering expeditions in South America. For further details of these guided expeditions please write or fax the above address.

# VENEZUELA AND COLOMBIA

## INTRODUCTION

The Andes of Venezuela and Colombia are lower than the great ranges further south and a high plateau is generally absent. The mountains often rise directly from the tropical lowlands, and this partly explains the bad weather prevalent in this part of the Andes. However the changes in vegetation zones as you climb are a fascinating feature of this area. Most ascents start in thick forest at 1500-2000m, cross mist shrouded moorland (known as páramo) at 3-4000m and finish on snow and ice. Particularly attractive are the frailejone plants which grow on the páramo.

At present (late 1996) Colombia is not a safe destination due to guerrilla violence, kidnappings and other crime. Only experienced travellers well aware of the risks should consider going to the country until the situation improves - **travel to any of the mountain areas of Colombia is not advisable**.

## GETTING THERE

There are flights from London and other major European cities to Caracas and Bogotá with the national airlines VIASA and Avianca (not London). While cheap, these airlines are not renowned for their service or reliability. Air France, KLM and Iberia also fly regularly to both cities at reasonable prices. British Airways are more expensive. From North America there are many daily flights to Caracas and Bogotá from Miami and New York as well as direct services from Miami to Cali and Barranquilla in Colombia.

For Merida in Venezuela an internal flight from Caracas is recommended, though the roads and buses are good. For the Colombian ranges it is probably best to acclimatise and buy supplies in Bogotá before flying on to your chosen area. Fly to Bucaramanga for the S. N. de Cocuy, Cali for Huila and Barranquilla for the S. N. de Santa Marta. (There are a few flights to Valledupar). The Los Nevados range are near enough to Bogotá to be reached comfortably by bus. For the other areas this is also an option for those short of funds. Roads and buses are generally good in Colombia but crime is a problem.

## SEASON

The weather is almost uniformly wet and tropical. The driest season and the best time to climb is November to April with January usually the best month. A shorter less pronounced dry spell is also possible in July. However there can be rain and storms at any time in all these ranges. Temperatures fall below freezing at night above about 4000m in the January dry season.

## CLIMBING CONDITIONS

Glaciers are generally small and crevasses present few problems. The snow is usually soft for most of the day in the dry season. Many routes involve a fair amount of rock scrambling and frequent overnight falls of snow can make these routes tricky.

The weather can be poor, even in the dry season and many summits will cloud over early every day e.g. 11a.m. In the wet season fresh snow and very poor weather make ascents difficult.

## OTHER GUIDE BOOKS

Expediciones a la Sierra Nevada de Merida, Chalbaud, Ediciones Paraguacocha, 1959.
Hiking/Backpacking in the Venezuelan Andes, Leighty, ISBN 0-9632950-0-4.

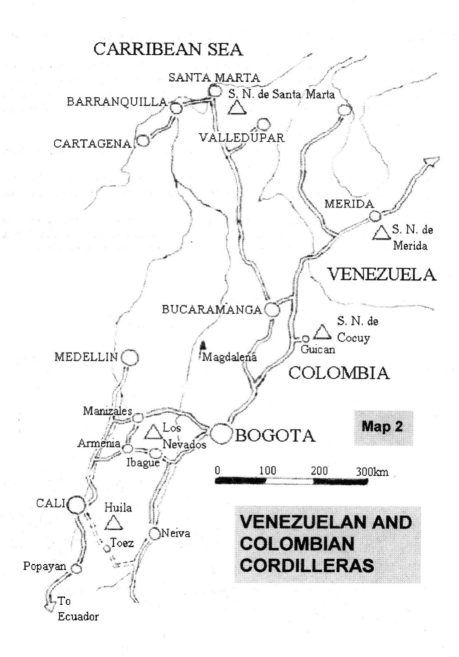

**Map 2**

0    100    200    300km

**VENEZUELAN AND
COLOMBIAN
CORDILLERAS**

# MERIDA   The principal city of the Venezuelan Andes          1574m

Merida is a small and pleasant city lying at the foot of the Sierra Nevada, the highest part of the Venezuelan Andes and the only area with permanent snow. To the N of the city lie the lower Cordillera del Norte with many easy peaks up to 4700m high. There is a large student population in the city and the nights can be lively. The authorities are not keen on solo climbers - if you are not in a group you may experience difficulties.

**FOOD** There are plenty of supermarkets in the central area.

**FUEL** Camping Gas from Remate Panama near corner of Calle 23 - Avenida 2. Kerosene from petrol stations around town.

**MOUNTAIN TRANSPORT** The cable car is the best and easiest option. It leaves from the centre of town (S end of Calle 25) in the mornings. Booking recommended. For Mucuy and other nearby roadheads just use a city taxi.

**MOUNTAIN INFORMATION** From the Teleferico (cable car) Station in Merida or from several tourist agencies nearby. Mountaineers must also register their plans at the station before going into the mountains. Also try Montaña at Edif. Las Americas, Avenida Las Americas.

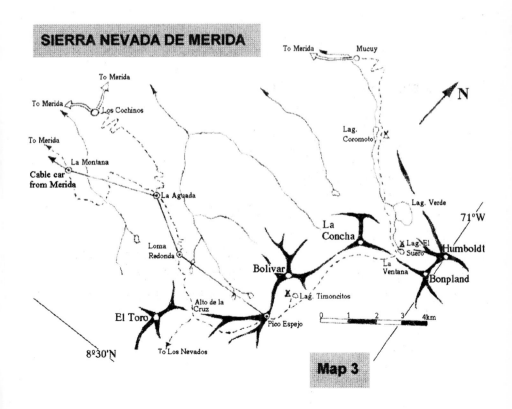

SIERRA NEVADA DE MERIDA

Map 3

# Po. BOLIVAR   5007m                Map 3                3 days   AD+

The highest peak in Venezuela, perhaps rather optimistically given a height of 5007m. Pico Bolivar is named after the liberator of South America, Simon Bolivar, who was born in Venezuela. A giant bust of him sits on the small summit of the peak. There are several small and basic refuges in the mountains but it is not wise to rely on getting space.

**ACCESS**   Easiest using the cable car from central Merida which used to go to **Pico Espejo 4768m,** but since an accident in 1991 only runs to the Loma Redonda station at 4000m (it might be repaired eventually). Going high on the cable car allows little acclimatisation and it may be better to walk at least some of the way. There are two main possibilities.   **1.** Walk all or part of the route of the cable car.  An easily followed path leaves from La Pueblita across the river from the cable car station or from the road at Los Cochinos.  Once at the Pico Espejo station walk NE along the flank of Bolivar to a high camp at Lag. Timoncitos (4750m). 2h. A steep down-climb on the direct route can be avoided by a longer and lower traverse.   **2.** Alternatively from the ranger station at Mucuy (2300m) follow the path through forest up the valley to SE - a trail is normally cut - ask for directions. Some scrambling higher up. This leads past the Lag. Coromoto (3300m - nice camps) and the Lag. Verde (4000m) to the rocky col known as  La Ventana (4500m). From here a traverse, with a slight drop, (called La Travesia) can be made along the S flank of Bolivar to reach Lag. Timoncitos. 3d.

**CLIMB**   The normal route is known as Ruta Weiss after the first ascensionist. This is a rock scramble mostly II but with a section of IV and very exposed near summit. This route follows the prominent gully sometimes containing snow on L of face above Lag. Timoncitos. This is climbed going L at half height, up a chimney to gain SW ridge. Then move onto NW face and up ledges to the summit. 4h.

**OTHER ROUTES**   There are several other routes on Bolivar. **1.** Ruta Bourgoin. From Lag. Timoncitos  go up the LHS of the snowfields above (there was a glacier here that has all but disappeared). Then traverse R towards the wide couloir known as the Garganta Bourgoin. Climb this and follow the ridge W to the summit. Harder than Ruta Weiss.   **2.** N face, Ruta Vinci. Make a rising traverse under N face of Espejo from Loma Redonda to gain  W glacier. Climb this to join the final part of the Ruta Weiss on NW face

**OTHER PEAKS** A fine rock scramble is **Pico El Toro 4755m,** best climbed from the Loma Redonda cable car station.  Follow path to Alto de la Cruz pass, then turn R towards the W and pass under S slopes of Toro. Scramble to the summit including a vertical chimney. 1d. The traverse from Toro SW to **Pico Leon 4746m,** is a classic exposed scramble.

**BEST MAP**   Parque Nacional Sierra Nevada - Mapa para excursionistas, 1:50,000, or 'Andes Centrales de Venezuela' approx. 1:50,000 both available in Merida from tourist shops etc.

# Po. HUMBOLDT   4942m          Map 3          3 days PD/AD

The second highest peak in the Sierra Nevada de Merida, about 6km E of Bolivar. Humboldt is the northern of two peaks known as La Corona, after the glacier on their NW slopes. It is named after the famous naturalist. The normal base camp is by the beautiful blue Lag. Suero.

**ACCESS**  By either of the routes described for Bolivar to a camp at Lag. El Suero. Either way will be one long day or two short days from Merida.

**CLIMB**  Go round the R of Lag. Suero and follow the stream up. Climb through buttresses - III in places. Then climb to the L of glacier until blocked by cliff. Go on to the glacier here and move up and R to the crest between Humboldt and Bonpland. (30°). Follow the crest NE to summit.

**OTHER PEAKS**  Humboldt's twin peak **Pico Bonpland 4883m,** can be climbed the same day as Humboldt. Follow the route for Humboldt onto the Corona glacier but then bear R to join the NE ridge of Bonpland. Some further rock climbing, grade n/k.

**BEST MAP**  As for Pico Bolivar.

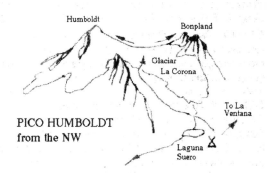

PICO HUMBOLDT
from the NW

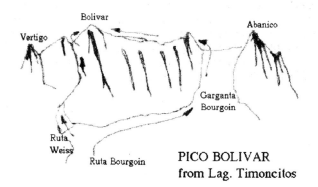

PICO BOLIVAR
from Lag. Timoncitos

# BOGOTÁ    The capital city of Colombia                    2650m

The capital of Colombia is a huge city which because of its height has a fairly cool climate. It is a city of both marked prosperity in the northern suburbs and terrible poverty in the southern barrios. Like many South American cities the centre can be roughly divided into old and new districts. Few streets in Bogotá have names. Numbers are used instead to identify the Calles and Carreras. This is also true of many other Colombian cities.

**SIGHTS** There are plenty of cultural sights to see - the usual mix of museums, churches and cathedrals surrounding Plaza de Bolivar. **Co. de Monserrate 3200m** to the E can be ascended by funicular, cable car or on foot for a good view of Bogotá. There is some good rock climbing at Suesca about one hour N of the city.

**MOUNTAIN INFORMATION** Try the Central Nacional de Montana, at Transversal 10 number 106-35, Bogotá. There's a nice cafe here too. The national park authority Inderena no longer exists. Permits for all national parks are now available from Ecoturismo, Carrera 13 #93-40 Oficina 401 (tel. 6233075).

**MOUNTAIN EQUIPMENT** As above or try the shop Almacen Aventura at Carrera 13, No. 67-26, Bogotá.

**FUEL** Camping Gas and some equipment can be bought at Casa Olimpica, Calle 17, No. 6-12.

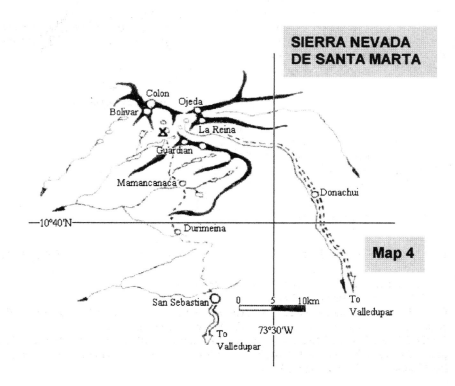

SIERRA NEVADA
DE SANTA MARTA

Map 4

## Po. CRISTOBAL COLON 5773m  Map 4            7 days  F/PD
## Po. SIMON BOLIVAR 5775m    Map 4            7 days  N/K

These neighbouring peaks in the Sierra Nevada de Santa Marta are the two highest peaks in Colombia. They are sometimes quoted with identical heights but in fact Bolivar is slightly higher. The Sierra Nevada de Santa Marta is a range which rises directly from the Caribbean and is technically not part of the Andean chain. Cristobal Colon is the Spanish name for Christopher Columbus, Simon Bolivar was the liberator of South America.

The local Arhuaco Indians are at times hostile - a local guide is often essential for safe passage. Reports are that all access to the mountains was forbidden in 1996. A permit is certainly necessary from the Casa Indigena just outside Valledupar. From the city of Valledupar get to either San Sebastian or (probably better) Donachui. 4WD may be needed. From either of these villages with local Indian guides and mules to the Lag. Nabobo base camp (4450m) which lies SE of the two peaks. All food and fuel should be brought from Valledupar.

**COLON CLIMB**   From the camp go N then R past two lakes then head direct for the SE side of Colon, to a high camp at edge of snowline (5000m). Climb the glacier keeping close to E face of Bolivar then climb up to the col between the peaks called La Horqueta (5500m). Then easily to the top of Colon, 5h., from high camp.

**BOLIVAR CLIMB**  Bolivar is normally climbed from La Horqueta too. It is harder than Colon, probably about AD and mostly on snow. Both can be climbed from the N too.
**BEST MAP**  CIGM sheets 19, 20, 26, 27 1:100,000

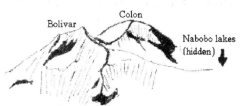

COLON and BOLIVAR from the S

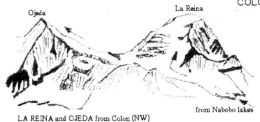

LA REINA and OJEDA from Colon (NW)

from Nabobo lakes

## Po. LA REINA 5735m           Map 4                    7 days  N/K

The third main peak of the Sierra Nevada de Santa Marta.
**ACCESS**  As for Colon and Bolivar above.
**CLIMB**   From the Naboba lakes base camp the normal route is via the large glacier on the N slopes. Grade n/k but probably about PD/AD. About 5h. from the lakes.
**OTHER PEAKS**  SE of the Nabobo Lakes is **El Guardián 5285m**, the most difficult of the big peaks. The easier **Pico Ojeda 5490m**, just to the N of La Reina, is normally climbed from the S.
**BEST MAP**   CIGM sheet as for Bolivar.

## RITACUBA BLANCO    5493m        Map 5                2 days  N/K

Ritacuba Blanco is the highest point of the Sierra Nevada del Cocuy, a beautiful mist enshrouded range with a reputation for bad weather. The range consists of two parallel chains running N-S. The W and more accessible chain is higher. Both chains rise gently on the W side and drop steeply on the E. A beautiful trek circles the mountains in 6-7 days.

**ACCESS**  From Bogotá either fly via the city of Bucaramanga or go direct by bus to Guicán (PT)(2900m). Guicán has a few shops and hotels. Maps available either here or in the town of Cocuy. From Guicán a jeep can be hired to get to Las Cabañas.

**CLIMB**  From Guicán to the hamlet of Las Cabañas then up the long W ridge on a fair trail to reach the glacier. Ascend easy glacier slopes then exposed ridge to summit. 1d from Las Cabañas. Grade probably about F or PD.

**BEST MAP**  CIGM sheets 137 'El Cocuy' and 153 'Chita'

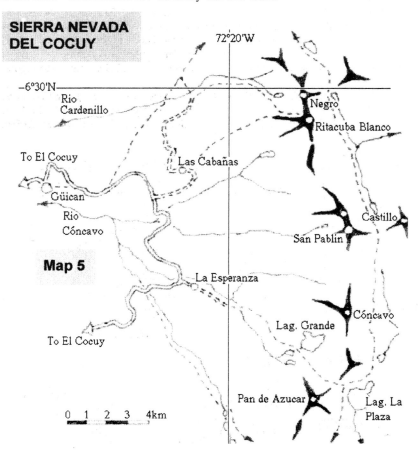

## No. DEL RUIZ  5305m          Map 6          1 day      F
## No. DEL TOLIMA  5274m        Map 6          3 days     F

These are the two highest peaks of a group of peaks commonly called Los Nevados. No. del Ruiz erupted in 1985 and a mudslide killed thousands in the town of Armero, over 50km away. There were also minor eruptions in 1996. Tolima is a symmetrical cone which last erupted in 1943. It is possible to combine the mountains by traversing the high páramo between them. Different heights are often quoted for mountains in this range.

**DEL RUIZ ACCESS**   From the city of Manizales (2150m) transport can be arranged to the park entrance at 4050m, just S of the Manizales to Murillo road. Check at Inderena office, C 20A, No 21-45 or the tourist office in Manizales about access to the national park. With good conditions and a 4WD it is possible to continue S up the road to within 2km of snowline to the ruins of a refugio (4790m).

**TOLIMA ACCESS**   For Tolima easiest access is from Ibagué (1250m) via the villages of Juntas and El Silencio (small shop) Then walk up the valley to the El Rancho hot spring on S side of mountain at 2600m - a beautiful spot with some food and accommodation.

**DEL RUIZ CLIMB**   From either the park entrance or the hut climb the NW glacier with only a few small crevasses to the highest visible point then over several rounded domes to the highest summit. 1d from entrance.

**TOLIMA CLIMB**  From El Rancho climb the muddy trail up the valley to get to La Cueva just above the treeline (3800m) (poor refugio). 4h. Continue on up NW over páramo to the large cross at Latas (4450m). 3h. Camping and water. Head direct to summit, snowline at 4800m, snow steep at first then easy. 4h. Some small crevasses.

**OTHER PEAKS**   Best climbed starting from Cidral to the W are **No. El Quindio 5150m,** F climbed from the pass 4410m by the NE ridge and **No. Santa Isabel 5100m,** F which is usually climbed from the N or W but can also be climbed from Lag. Otun to the SW.

**BEST MAP**   CIGM sheets 206, 225, 244 1:100,000

**Map 6**

**LOS NEVADOS**

## No. DEL HUILA  5365m                Map 7                6 days  N/K

This peak is the highest point of the Cordillera Central. It consists of four summits in a roughly N-S line. The highest point is known as Mayor towards the S of the range and shows some signs of activity. The often quoted height of 5750m is almost certainly an exaggeration.

**ACCESS**    From the city of Cali to Toez (PT) where there are some shops. The trail starts about 25km N of Toez and leaves the road 3km N of the Inderena hut (2910m). From the road climb up the Q. Verdun to the NE through forest (a guide and a few machetes will be useful) for about 2½km then turn S and head up steeply at first onto the páramo. Then head generally SE towards the mountains to snowline at about 4400m. High camp on glacier at 4600m. 2d.

**CLIMB**    The ordinary route is on the W face over glaciers. Grade n/k.

**OTHER PEAKS**    The next peak N **Pico La Cresta 5100,** is a difficult mixed climb by S ridge. Probably AD or higher.

**BEST MAP**    No good maps available.

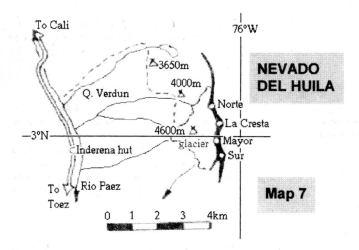

# ECUADOR

## INTRODUCTION
Ecuador has been a very popular destination for mountaineers travelling to South America ever since Whymper climbed in the famous 'Avenue of the Volcanoes' at the end of last century. The fame of mountains such as Chimborazo and Cotopaxi surpasses their importance in the Andes as a whole. In reality the Andes of Ecuador are a small fraction of the what the continent has to offer.

The volcanoes of Ecuador are generally very busy mountains and the climate in Ecuador could best be described as very variable and not ideal for mountaineering. The mountains will be something of a disappointment to more experienced mountaineers. For novices they are ideal - they are very accessible and provide relatively easy ascents to high altitude. With a base in the capital Quito most peaks can be climbed in a 'long weekend'. There are huts on almost all the high peaks.

## GETTING THERE
There are flights from several European countries direct to the capital Quito (Air France, KLM, Iberia and Lufthansa all fly there). From London you will need to change either in Europe or in Caracas or Bogotá. There are many direct flights to Quito from Miami and a few from Los Angeles.

## SEASON
The weather patterns are very complicated with two dry seasons; June to July and December to January. Neither of these seasons is perfectly dry and climbs can be successful at other times of year. The period to avoid at all costs is the very wet March to May.

The eastern peaks are particularly affected by the proximity of the Amazon basin and Antisana, El Altar and Sangay suffer very wet climates. These peaks are best in December to February. The western peaks are driest from June to August but also have a short dry season around December. These western peaks are very wet from February to April. Cotopaxi, surrounded by the other peaks is noticeably drier than most.

## CLIMBING CONDITIONS
Ecuador gets lots of wet snow so climbs are often in heavy snow. Whenever you climb the weather is likely to be unreliable and a very early start should be made to reach the summit soon after first light. Cloud often builds on the summits as early as 10a.m.

Refuges can be very busy at weekends due to the easy access and the popularity of climbing in Ecuador. Most have basic facilities i.e. water, WC, cooking facilities and bunks, but you'll need a sleeping bag and food.

## OTHER GUIDE BOOKS
Bradt Publications, Climbing and Hiking in Ecuador, 3rd Ed. 1994.
Montañas del Sol, Serrano-Rojas-Landazuri, Ediciones Campo Abierto, Quito, 1994.

## QUITO   The capital of Ecuador and an excellent base          2800m

The capital of Ecuador is a beautifully situated city with views to the snow capped volcanoes Cotopaxi and Cayambe. It was the northern capital of the Inca Empire at the time of the Spanish conquest. Though no trace of the Incas remain, many beautiful Spanish colonial buildings can be seen in the old town, parts of which have been designated as a world heritage site. At an altitude of 2800m and with all facilities within easy reach the city is the only sensible base for climbing the volcanoes of Ecuador.

**SIGHTS**   There are the usual mixture of museums in the city and a few km N the Equator can be visited in a half day trip. The crater at Pululagua is also worth seeing while acclimatising. Rising above Quito to the W is **Rucu Pichincha 4787m, F** which makes a fine day out for the acclimatised. Take a taxi to Cruz Loma, climb by the SE ridge (lots of enjoyable but avoidable scrambling up to III) then descend to Quito in one day.

**Guagua Pichincha 4794m, F** further W makes a longer excursion.

**FOOD**   There is a good choice of supermarkets in the new part of town.

**FUEL**   Kerosene from petrol stations around town, camping gas from various sports and mountain equipment retailers around town (see below).

**MOUNTAIN INFO**   Try the South American Explorers Club recently moved to Jorge Washington 311 or the Nuevos Horizontes Club at Colon 2038. The Gran Casino Hotel still seems to be the best place to meet up with other climbers.

**MOUNTAIN TRANSPORT AND EQUIPMENT** For private transport and to hire or buy equipment try one of the following agencies: Agama Expediciones, Venezuela 1163, Alta Montaña, Jorge Washington 425, Andean Sport, Roca 549 or Sierra Nevada, Juan Leon Mera 741.

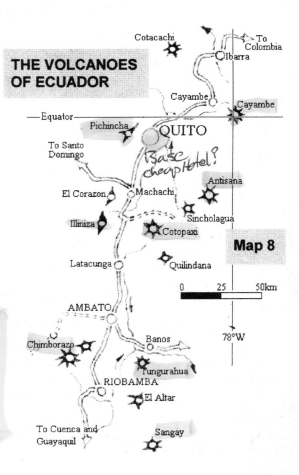

THE VOLCANOES OF ECUADOR

Map 8

*Best w/Partner*

# CAYAMBE  5790m

Map 8

3 days   PD

Cayambe is a more difficult mountain than either Chimborazo or Cotopaxi. It is renowned for bad weather, big crevasses and avalanches and also for being the highest mountain in the world actually on the equator.

**ACCESS**   From Quito to Cayambe town. 1km S of Cayambe town take a 4WD cobbled road to Piemonte Bajo (3500m). Turn L here and continue to the refuge on the SW slopes (4600m), good facilities but no food. 25km. Some of this route may have to be walked if the road is in poor condition or your driver is timid.

**CLIMB**   Climb the rocky ridge behind the refuge and directly on to glacier. Climb N past rock outcrops. Just before reaching a larger cliff turn E towards the summit (bergschrund) and climb through steep snow flutings. 9h.

**OTHER ROUTES**   The old route from the N joins the normal route at the rock outcrops.

**OTHER PEAKS**   SE of Cayambe is **Sara Urcu, 4676m**  reached by taking R turn at Piemonte Bajo and walking about 40km. Climbed easily by glacier and SW ridge. 6d.

**BEST MAP**   EIGM sheet 3994-II 'Cayambe' and 4094-III 'Nevado Cayambe' both 1:50,000

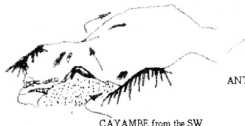

summit

Antisanilla

ANTISANA  normal route  SW side

CAYAMBE from the SW

*Probably PD*

# ANTISANA  5704m

Map 9

4 days  N/K

An active but no longer conical volcano. The central summit is the highest. The hardest of the four big summits in Ecuador.

**ACCESS**   From Pintag  (2850m) (PT) go S on 4WD track to Hac. Pinantura, soon after turn L for Hac. Antisana (4100m). 34km. Drive another 8km to the road end. From here walk NE to a base camp on snowline at 4600m. 1h. The mountain can also be approached from Lag. Papallacta to the N, recent reports of access problems at the Hac. Pinantura may make this northern approach preferable.

**CLIMB**   Head up glacier towards lowest point of ridge joining central and S summits. Just before ridge turn L and follow glacier slope N avoiding crevasses. The summit is surrounded by a big crevasse and a long traverse (R or L depending on the year) may be needed to cross it. Grade n/k but probably AD. 7h.

**OTHER ROUTES**   The S peak, sometimes called Antisanilla, can be climbed from a high glacier camp on the normal route.  Mixed rock and ice.  For a detailed description see Bradt guide.

**BEST MAP**   EIGM 'Pintag' 1:100,000

**ILLINIZA** Sur  5263m            Map 9                3 days  AD
**ILLINIZA** Norte  5126m          Map 9                3 days  PD

The S peak of the twin Illiniza peaks is a steep and glaciated summit, often quite difficult. The N peak is a relatively straightforward rock scramble. Both peaks can be climbed from a refuge in the col which separates them.

**ACCESS**    From Quito to the town of Machachi then to the small village of El Chaupi (3350m)(PT). A deteriorating 4WD track continues from here to about 4200m. It goes W for about 3km then turns L and goes SW up the ridge on the S side of the Q. Cachanguvi, turning sooner or later into a path up the sandy ridge which leads to the refuge (no facilities) at 4650m beneath the col which separates the peaks. 6h walk from El Chaupi.

**ILLINIZA SUR CLIMB**    From the refuge head W into the saddle. Halfway there turn L to gain the glacier. Here there is a large plateau. Cross this almost all the way to the W to reach the NE flank of the mountain. Climb this by a series of canaletas. 6h. Ice to 50°.  The more direct route formerly used as the normal route is more difficult.

**ILLINIZA NORTE CLIMB** Illiniza Norte can also be climbed from the refuge. From the col climb up  easy slopes to gain the SE ridge of the N peak which is an exciting rock scramble with a gendarme half way up. To reach summit skirt this on the R, make a rising traverse under the buttresses beneath the summit then head back L. 3-4h.

**OTHER PEAKS**    To the N is **El Corazon 4788m**  climbed by the N ridge from a saddle on the N side, some easy scrambling. 4h. Start at a characteristic pinewood reached by dirt track from Aloasi, a village  which lies 4km W of Machachi.

**BEST MAP**    EIGM  sheet 3892-II, 'Machachi' 1:50,000

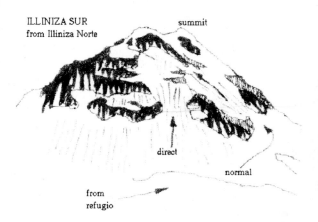

ILLINIZA SUR
from Illiniza Norte

summit

direct

normal

from
refugio

Photo: **Frailejone plants beneath Pico Bolivar, Venezuela.** M. Shaw collection

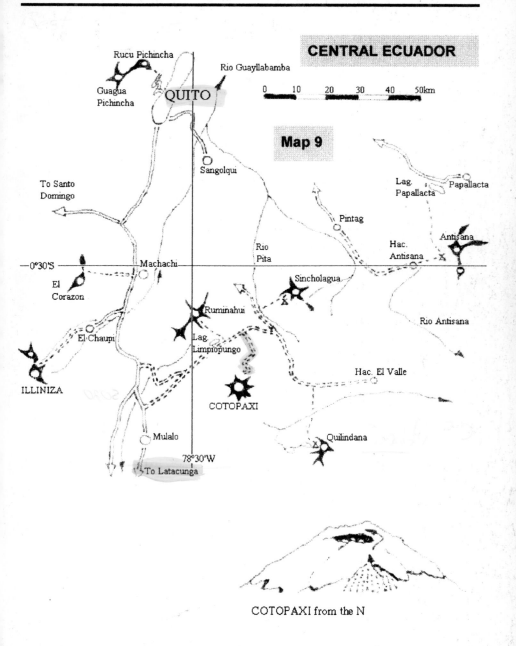

COTOPAXI from the N

Photo: **Starting the Ferrari route, Alpamayo, Cordillera Blanca, Peru**. D. Bearhop collection

## COTOPAXI  5897m                    Map 9                    3 days    F

Cotopaxi is a spectacular heavily glaciated volcanic cone, seen on the skyline from Quito. The mountain is often wrongly claimed to be the world's highest active volcano, but several peaks in northern Chile and southern Peru are higher and (at least currently) more active. The volcano was very active from  the 1850's to 1870's. The volcano now forms the centrepiece to one of Ecuador's most famous national parks. The normal route is on the N side.

**ACCESS**    Nearest PT is at the park entrance station on the Pan American highway about 20km due W of the volcano. In the nearest town of Latacunga  jeeps or pickups can be hired for the rough drive up to the parking area below the refuge which is ½h  directly up hill at 4600m. The refuge has WC and bunkbeds and usually has cooking facilities but no food.

**CLIMB**    From the hut go to top of triangular scree slope to gain glacier. Move up and R around large crevasses passing the huge rockband (known as Yanasacha and clearly seen even from Quito) on the R. Then move back L and up slightly steeper snow to summit crater. 7h.

**OTHER PEAKS**    17km NE of Cotopaxi is **Sincholagua, 4893m**. The  normal route is on the SW rock ridge. 2d. The route is easy to find and not difficult. 13km NW of Cotopaxi is **Rumiñahui, 4712m, F**. The highest N peak can be climbed by the furthest N big gully of reddish sand on the E face. 6h from Limpiopungo. To the S **Quilindaña, 4878m, about AD** can be climbed from a high camp at the small lake to the NW (4350m). From here climb the couloir to the NW ridge. Climb ridge direct on good rock IV-V. 2d.

**BEST MAP**  EIGM sheets 3992-III 'Sincholagua' and 3991-IV 'Cotopaxi' both 1:50,000.

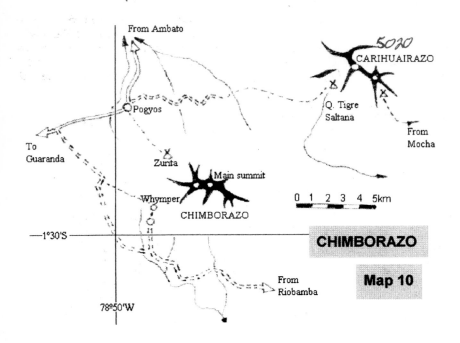

# CHIMBORAZO 6310m        Map 10        4 days        F

The highest peak in Ecuador and for a long time thought to be the highest peak in the world. Due to the earth's equatorial bulge, Chimborazo does in fact have the distinction that its summit is further from the centre of the earth than any other point.

Two routes are commonly climbed. The normal (Whymper) route from the large refuges on the SW face and the NW face or Pogyos route, which will need a camp. Which route is easier varies from year to year depending on the state of the glacier. Due to the receding glaciers the Whymper route now goes L from the hut.

**ACCESS**    1.   For the Whymper route drive all the way to the refuge (4800m) at the road end by taxi from Riobamba via San Juan. There is another refuge, called the Whymper refuge at 5000m. You can also walk to these two refuges from the Ambato - Guaranda road which lies to the NE (PT). Get off the bus about 5km beyond Pogyos at a white house at a pass (4200m). 4-5h.    2.   For the NW face leave the Guaranda - Ambato road (PT) at the shacks at Pogyos (4000m). Mules can be hired here for the 3h trip up NW slopes of mountain to the ruined Zurita hut (4900m). No water.

**CLIMB**    1.   For the normal route from the Whymper refuge climb NW up scree to gain the glacier by a large shelf below the prominent rock known as Castillo. Climb the glacier to the ridge above. Climb the ridge heading NW to the Veintimilla summit. The main summit is due E and 1km away across the plateau (often soft snow later in day). 8h. The direct start to the Whymper route is more difficult and dangerous.    2.   From the ruined Zurita hut go up scree then snow to the large red rock. Traverse R then go straight up to the Veintimilla summit. Continue to the main summit as for 1 above. 8h.

**OTHER ROUTES**    From camps on the E side of Chimborazo the prominent rock formation Piedra Negra can be climbed, IV. The E summit of Chimborazo (called Martinez 5570m) can be climbed by the Moreno glacier on the E flank, turning a rock outcrop high up by the SE. There is also a fine mixed route to this summit (Arista del Sol). For a detailed description see either Montañas del Sol or the Bradt guide. The integral traverse (E-W) was first done in 1980 and will require 3-4d.

**OTHER PEAKS**    To the NE is **Carihuairazo 5020m, F.**    Approach from Ambato - Guaranda road (PT) to a camp at the head of the Q. Tigre Saltana valley (4700m). 5h. Go R to gain SW ridge. Follow this turning an outcrop on the L then up glacier (few crevasses) and on to summit, 3h.

**BEST MAP** EIGM, sheet 3889-IV 'Chimborazo' 1:50,000. Also sheet 3889-I 'Quero' for Carihuairazo

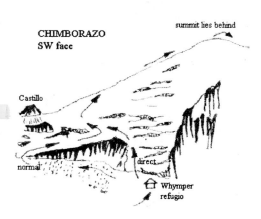

CHIMBORAZO
SW face

summit lies behind

Castillo

normal

direct

Whymper
refugio

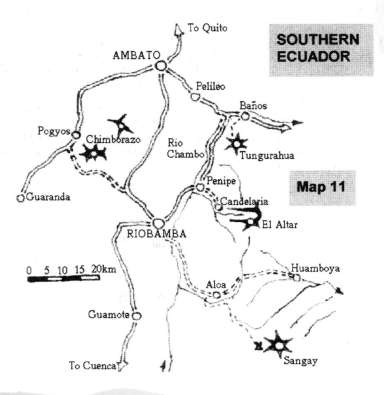

## TUNGURAHUA 5023m          Map 11          3 days     F

An active volcano on the edge of the Amazon basin. A few fumaroles and steam vents can be seen on route to the summit.

**ACCESS**   From Quito to the small town of Baños (1800m)(PT) via Ambato. Drive from Baños 1km out of town towards Ambato then turn L for the small village of Pondoa where mules are often available. Continue by a very muddy path with some interesting bamboo tunnels to the refugio at the treeline on the N rib of the mountain (3800m). 4h from Pondoa.

**CLIMB**    Set off very early - proximity of Amazon basin means cloud gathers early.
Follow the rib with no difficulties but occasional sections of scree or very easy scrambling. Crampons and axe needed for summit snowfield but no crevasses. About 5h.

**BEST MAP**   EIGM,   sheet 3989-IV, 'Volcan Tungurahua'  1:25,000

*Possible w/Partner*

**ALTAR** 5319m               Map 12               6 days  AD/D

Altar is the only big peak in Ecuador whose ascent is technically difficult and indeed the first ascent of the highest point was not until 1963. The mountain is a massive blown out crater with steep walls on three sides and a number of pinnacles around the crater rim, the highest of which is known as El Obispo. The climate is very wet. The name is Spanish and means altar. The native Quechua name for the mountain is Capac Urcu

**ACCESS**    From Quito by Riobamba or Ambato to village of Peñipe (PT) then by truck for 10km to Candelaria (3000m). Small store and mules here. Cross the bridge and go 2km to the park entrance. Walk up hill and past Hac. Releche then after 45 minutes take a faint trail L and up to join a clear track. Follow this easily S and then E up the Rio Blanco to a camp at the entrance to the crater. 7h. from Candelaria.

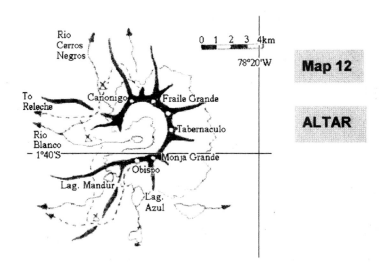

**OBISPO CLIMB**   From the crater camp cross the ridge to the S and drop down to Lag. Mandur then up the black ridge to the S (possible camp). Then go N to gain the lower glacier above Lag. Azul. Climb wide and obvious gully to upper glacier. Traverse R and climb steep narrow gully to summit ridge. Go R and climb 30m rock band on rotten rock (IV-V)

**OTHER ROUTES**   From a base camp at Rio Cos. Negros to the N of the mountain the 2nd highest peak **El Canonigo 5260m,** can be climbed. Traverse NE glacier to reach small ridge leading to minor E summit. Difficult mixed climbing from here up to summit. **Monja Grande 5160m,** the next peak E of El Obispo can be climbed from the col joining it to Obispo, gained from the S glacier.

**BEST MAP**   None available.

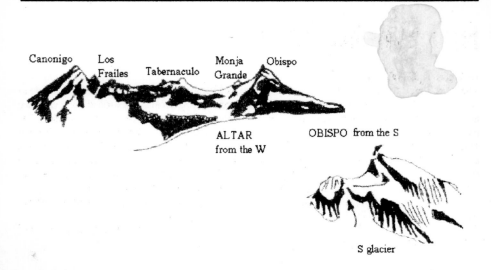

Canonigo    Los          Monja    Obispo
            Frailes  Tabernaculo  Grande

ALTAR
from the W

OBISPO from the S

S glacier

## SANGAY  5230m                    Map 11              8 days  PD

About 40km S of El Altar is the dangerously active volcano, Sangay. It lies in an isolated area of
country SW of Riobamba and suffers a very wet climate. The grade of PD is probably justified
due to the extreme objective danger from the barrage of large lava bombs. The name is Quechua
and means the frightener.

**ACCESS**  From the village of Alao (PT) it is essential to hire a guide to get you through difficult
forest terrain to a camp at La Playa SW of the peak. 3d.

**CLIMB**  Climbing is reputedly safest by the S slopes but active volcanoes change fast!
Crampons and axe may be necessary depending on the state of the snow but there are no
crevasses. The volcano spits out ten ton boulders so watch out!

**BEST MAP**  none available

# NORTHERN PERU

## INTRODUCTION
The two main ranges of Northern Peru, the Cordillera Blanca and the nearby Cordillera Huayhuash are undoubtedly the most spectacular and challenging of the Andean ranges. There are over 20 main 6000m summits, many of them amongst the hardest peaks in the Andes. The twin summits of Huascarán dominate the northern end of the Cord. Blanca and are the 5th and 10th highest peaks in the Andes. Yerupajá towers over the other peaks of the Huayhuash and is the 11th highest peak in the Andes. Also included in this section are several lower ranges inland from Lima with peaks up to 5700m high, collectively known as the Central Cordilleras. For mountaineers the Cord. Blanca have the added bonus of relatively easy access. Most base camps can be reached in a day from the towns of the large valley, called the Callejón de Huaylas, which lies to the W of the mountains. The main town in this valley is Huaraz.

Access to the Cord. Huayhuash is a little longer, with most base camps taking at least 2-3 days of trekking to reach from the principal access town of Chiquian.

## GETTING THERE
All areas are easiest to approach by flying to Lima, the capital of Peru. From Europe there are direct flights from Madrid (Iberia), Amsterdam (KLM) and Frankfurt (Lufthansa). There are no direct flights from London so a change in Europe or a flight via Miami, Bogotá or Caracas will be necessary. From the USA there are many direct flights from Miami and a few from LA, with either United, American or the Peruvian carriers Faucett and AeroPeru.

Get out of Lima as soon as you can - it's a damp and depressing city in the climbing season. From Lima the only practical way to Huaraz, the main city of the Cordillera Blanca, is by bus. This is an 8h journey. Most buses are reasonably comfortable and the road is now surfaced all the way. Watch out for thieves in Lima bus stations. There are flights from Lima to the airfield N of Huaraz but these are on a small plane with restricted baggage.

For the Cord. Huayhuash there are direct buses to Chiquian but it may be easier to go via Huaraz, particularly if you have food, mules etc. to sort out.

For the Central Cordilleras see individual entries for the best access. This will normally involve a bus journey direct from Lima, though there may be an advantage to basing yourself in the highland towns of La Oroya, Cerro de Pasco or Huancayo for the altitude advantage.

## SEASON
The climbing season extends from May to September, with June and July reckoned to be the best months. Though this is winter, it is the dry season in the mountains. The weather is generally very stable with normally only one or two bad days in a week. Freezing level is about 4500-5000m during the day, but strong sun can make it feel much warmer. Wind is rarely a problem in the dry season. Bad weather comes from the Amazon side of the mountains, from the E or the N.

## CLIMBING CONDITIONS
Ascents are mostly snow and ice routes. In general N faces tend to have very good snow and ice, S faces often have soft unconsolidated powder and E and W faces a mixture. Penitentes are present but not very common. Soft snow can be a problem above 5500m, but on many of the

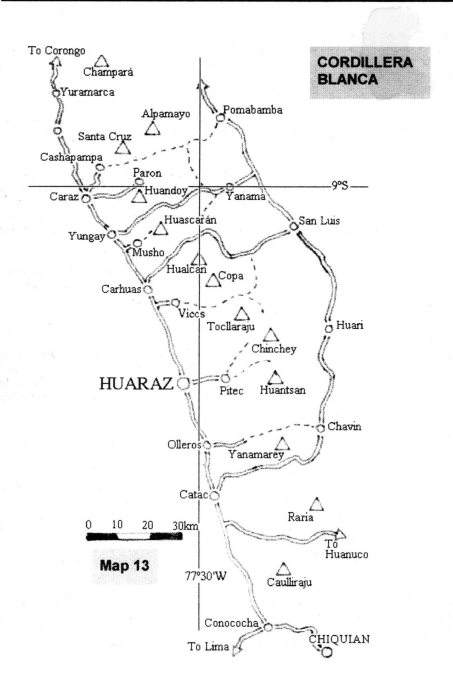

CORDILLERA BLANCA

To Corongo

Champará

Yuramarca

Alpamayo          Pomabamba

Santa Cruz

Cashapampa

Paron

Caraz    Huandoy          Yanama          —9°S—

Huascarán          San Luis

Yungay

Musho

Hualcán   Copa

Carhuas

Viccs

Tocllaraju          Huari

Chinchey

HUARAZ

Pitec    Huantsan

Chavin

Olleros

Yanamarey

Catac

Raria

0   10   20   30km                                    To
                                                      Huanuco
Map 13

77°30'W          Caulliraju

Conococha
To Lima          CHIQUIAN

more popular peaks someone else will have made a trail for you.

Ridges in this part of Peru are famous for being unstable and often doubly corniced, and therefore very difficult. Many are unjustifiably dangerous for the average expedition.

Snow avalanches are relatively rare in the climbing season but do occur at the start of the season and after heavy snowfall. Serac collapses can be a danger on many of the normal routes - watch where you camp.

Many of the routes change from year to year as the glaciers move and can be impassable to all but the most determined expeditions. Enquire locally if possible about current conditions

### OTHER GUIDE BOOKS

This is one of the few areas of the Andes with a fair number of guidebooks published. Sharman's definitive guide is certainly the best, particularly for details of modern harder lines. Brief details of such routes are given here but anyone wishing to climb such routes should buy Sharman's guide. Beaud's guide has some nice pictures but nothing else to recommend it. Yuraq Janka is a carefully researched listing  but is now a bit out of date and was never very effective as a guide book.

Climbs of the Cordillera Blanca of Peru, Sharman, 1995, ISBN 0-9523582-0-4

The Peruvian Andes, Beaud, pub. Cordee, 1988, covers the Cord. Blanca and Cord. Huayhuash.

Callejón de Huaylas y Cordillera Blanca, Diaz, pub. Kuntur, 1989, Spanish language, available in Huaraz, covers the Cord. Blanca and Cord. Huayhuash.

Yuraq Janka, Ricker, pub. American Alpine Club, 1977, covers the Cord. Blanca.

### MAPS

Names have mainly been taken from Felipe Diaz's map 'Cordilleras Blanca and Huayhuash' approx. 1:200,000. This is a very useful map which is available cheaply in Huaraz. The Alpenvereins maps are fairly good but glaciers and glacier lakes may be out of date. The PIGM maps use some unusual names that are not often understood locally. They are however more up to date and show better topographical detail in places.

# HUARAZ   The main town of the Cordillera Blanca   3090m

Huaraz sits at 3090m at the southern end of the Callejon de Huaylas and  makes an ideal base for the Cord. Blanca. It is a cheerful and relatively prosperous town. For mountaineers it has as many facilities as you'll get in Peru and most valley road heads can be reached in a couple of hours drive by private transport or less than a day by public transport. The town is a very active climbing centre in season with lots of gear shops and plenty of cafes and cheap hotels full of climbers looking for partners etc.

**SIGHTS**  The fascinating underground temple complex at Chavin is well worth a visit (take a torch) though this involves a 4h journey. Immediately above Huaraz are the ruins of Wilkawain, torch also necessary. Get a taxi up and walk back down as an acclimatisation day.

**FOOD**  There are no great one-stop shops in Huaraz. The shop on the corner of Luzuriaga and Raymondi has the best choice and there are a number of others in this area. Out of date Chilean and Argentine biscuits and chocolate can be bought on the stalls along Luzuriaga. The market area W of Luzuriaga  has a reasonable choice of fresh fruit and vegetables.

**FUEL**   The petrol station ('Grifo' - in Peru) on Raymondi just W of Luzuriaga sells petrol and kerosene. Camping Gas is usually available from several of the climbing and trekking agencies on Luzuriaga, but isn't cheap.

**MOUNTAIN INFO**   The best place to go for information on conditions is the Casa de Guias (guides office) in a quiet square just E of Luzuriaga behind the bank. If you want a partner try leaving a note either at the Casa de Guias or in Edward's Inn.

**MOUNTAIN EQUIPMENT**   Several shops along the main street (Luzuriaga) sell and rent equipment - you'll trip over the tents pitched on the pavement. As most of this is second-hand or dumped equipment don't expect good quality.

**MOUNTAIN TRANSPORT**   Many tour agencies up and down Luzuriaga will provide private transport and arrange donkey or porter services but try Pablo Tours, Luzuriaga 501 or Casa de Guias, Plaza Ginebra.

## No. CHAMPARÁ 5749m         Map 13              5 days N/K

A small isolated massif lying N of the main range. Very rarely visited.

**ACCESS**   From Huaraz to Yuramarca then to Hac. Mirasanta (2600m) lying W of the peaks. From here walk E up the steep Q. Coronguillo to reach the Lag. Qollurcocha (4000m) NW of the main peak.

**CLIMB**   From Lag. Qollurcocha ascend to a col (c.4900m) on W ridge then traverse steep N face (snow and ice) to reach summit.

**OTHER PEAKS**   Further N lie the Cord. Rosko, access is via Corongo. The highest peak called **Rosko Grande 5188m**, is normally climbed from NW. This area is even less often visited.

**BEST MAP**   As for Santa Cruz below.

## No. SANTA CRUZ 6259m       Map 14              6 days D+

A superb ice and granite pyramid also known as Pucaraju. The most commonly climbed line appears to be the W ridge. The name is Spanish for holy cross.

**ACCESS**   From Huaraz via Caraz to the village of Cashapampa (3000m) (PT). This is the start of many routes into the mountains and it is easy to arrange donkeys, find somewhere to sleep etc. For the W ridge walk via the village of Huancarhuaz and up to Lag. Yuraccocha (4600m). 1½d. For SW face and ridge routes, approach via Q. Rajucolta, (path on S side) to camp at lagoon by moraine (4650m). 1d.

**CLIMB  W ridge D+**.   From Yuraccocha climb S to the col overlooking Q. Rajucolta (5350m). Ascend the W ridge on snow slopes to a curved ice wall at 5800m. Pass this on the R and climb runnels (55-60°) to regain the ridge, then continue more easily to summit, 2-3d.

**OTHER ROUTES**   Other 'popular' routes include the **SW ridge, D+** joined from the RHS of SW face (55-60°) at an altitude of 5600m. The ridge is mixed ground at about 40°. Possible bivouac at 6100m. Also the **SW face, TD**. which climbs the L side of the face on 70° ice, turning a rock band capped by seracs on the L.

**BEST MAP**   Alpenvereinskarte sheet 0/3a 'Cordillera Blanca Nord' 1:100,000 or PIGM sheet 18-h 'Corongo' 1:100,000.

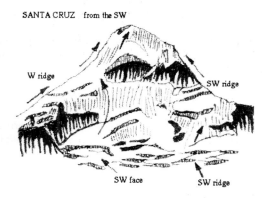

SANTA CRUZ from the SW

W ridge

SW ridge

SW face

SW ridge

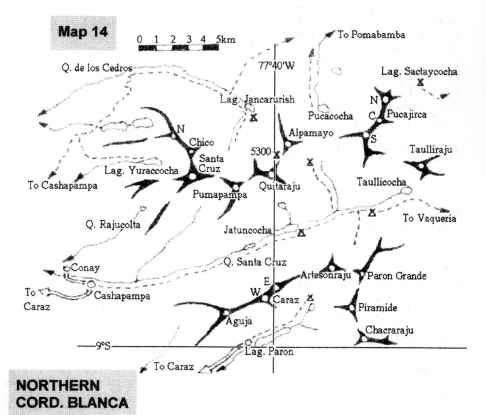

**Map 14**

0 1 2 3 4 5km

To Pomabamba

Q. de los Cedros

77°40'W

Lag. Sactaycocha

Lag. Jancarurish

Pucacocha

N

C Pucajirca

Chico

Alpamayo

S

N

5300

Taulliraju

Santa Cruz

Lag. Yuraccocha

To Cashapampa

Pumapampa

Quitaraju

Taullicocha

Q. Rajucolta

To Vaqueria

Jatuncocha

Q. Santa Cruz

Conay

Artesonraju

Paron Grande

To Caraz

Cashapampa

E

W

Caraz

Piramide

Aguja

Chacraraju

9°S

Lag. Paron

To Caraz

**NORTHERN CORD. BLANCA**

# QUITARAJU 6040m          Map 14          7 days   AD

Also spelt Kitaraju. Climbed quite frequently due mostly to the proximity of the more famous Alpamayo. The two peaks can be combined from a high camp (5300m) in the col which separates them. Allow 8-9 days for this.

**ACCESS**  From Huaraz to Cashapampa (3000m) (PT) then up the S side of Q. Santa Cruz and then Q. Arhuaycocha to the Alpamayo base camp, 2d. From here follow cairned path NW, then moraine crest to glacier edge, 2h. Continue by following cairns N then circle E up glacier to Alpamayo - Quitaraju col. This is gained by a 300m ramp (40° - stakes sometimes in situ), 3h. Camp just down the far side (5300m). This is the usual approach for both the W ridge and the N face as well as for Alpamayo.

**CLIMBS  W ridge, AD.** From the 5300m camp in the col traverse the glacier under the N slopes of Quitaraju and gain the Quitaraju - Loyacjirca col. Choose a route through the seracs of the N flank (to 60°). Climb the ridge more easily to the summit. 8h.

**N face, D-,**  Follow traverse above until under the N face then cross the bergschrund (5400m) just R of a rock rib (45-50°). Climb directly up to reach summit ridge about 80m W of summit. Anchors sometimes in place. Lines further R are prone to avalanche. 5h.

**BEST MAP**  As for Santa Cruz above.

QUITARAJU from the W

W ridge

N face

from 5300m camp

top out

summit

ALPAMAYO
SW face normal

camp
5300

# No. ALPAMAYO 5947m          Map 14          7 days  AD+

One of the world's most impressive and memorable mountains, Alpamayo is a steep fluted wedge of snow and ice. Most parties content themselves with a climb to the summit ridge because traversing to the true S summit is both difficult and serious. The Ferrari route on the SW face is very popular and there are usually belay/abseil points in place. The name is Quechua and means muddy river.

**ACCESS**  Follow the access to the 5300m camp on the Alpamayo - Quitaraju col detailed for Quitaraju above, 3d. This col can also be reached with more difficulty from the N. Approach from Cashapampa up the Q. de Los Cedros to the Lag. Jancarurish (c.4500m). Good camping, 3d. Climb the crevassed glacier to the col camp at 5300m. ½d.

**CLIMB    Ferrari route AD+.** From the 5300m camp cross easy slopes and climb to the bergschrund. Cross on a snow bridge just before the highest point is reached. Follow flutings slanting up R (45-50°, 350m) to reach the lowest point of summit ridge. 6-8h.

**OTHER ROUTES** Also on the SW face is the **French direct, D+** which climbs the 50-65° runnel which leads directly to the S summit. All the other runnels on the SW face have been climbed at grades to TD. All these routes now severely affected by a massive collapse of the lower RHS of the SW face.

Alpamayo can also be climbed from the N by the **N ridge, D** which was the route of the first ascent. From Lag. Jancarurish (4500m) climb towards the ridge through the ice fall (difficult route finding) to easy snow slopes at the foot of the ridge. Skirt a bergschrund and start up the ridge 45-50° which steepens with some mixed sections. The summit cornice may be very difficult (turn on L). This route can also be gained by traversing from the 5300 camp.

**OTHER PEAKS**   Lying about 7km E of Alpamayo is the spectacular **Taulliraju 5830m.** This is actually a subsidiary summit of the Pucajirca massif but is normally climbed from the Q. Santa Cruz side from a base camp at Taullicocha (4500m) near the head of the valley. There are a profusion of difficult (TD or ED) mixed routes on the SW face and a couple of easier lines on the N face as described in Sharman's guide.

**BEST MAP**   As for Santa Cruz above.

# PUCAJIRCA Norte  6046m          Map 14          8 days  N/K

Pucajirca or Pucahirca is a long chain of peaks lying E of Alpamayo. The highest point is at the N end. These are very quiet peaks for the Cordillera Blanca. The name means red mountain. The height is given as only 5943m on the PIGM map.

**ACCESS**   From Huaraz to the remote village of Pomabamba (3000m) on the E side of the range (PT). Walk up the Q. Jancapampa to the W, turn N at the head of this and climb the steeper Q. Yanajanca (Q. Laurel on PIGM) to a base camp at c.4000m by Lag. Sactaycocha.

**CLIMB**   The only recorded ascent was by the N ridge from Lag. Sactaycocha. Begin ascending the glacier descending into the valley SW of the lake, then traverse S and cross over the base of the E ridge (c.5000m) of the subsidiary summit immediately N of Pucahirca Norte. Climb the curving glacier which descends from the col between the main and subsidiary summits, first NW then SW up an icefall, to reach the col. Climb the N ridge. Final ascent from a camp at 5400m in 9h. Probably about D or TD.

**OTHER ROUTES**   The central and southern peaks have been climbed from Q. Santa Cruz at grades of D or TD (see Sharman).

**BEST MAP**   As for Santa Cruz and PIGM sheet 18-i useful for access.

# No. CARAZ Oeste  6025m        Map 14              4 days  PD

Caraz Oeste is the highest of a group of peaks on the N side of Lag. Paron. The peak is one of the easiest 6000'ers in the range. Approaches are normally made from the S by Lag. Paron. Climbing from Q. Santa Cruz to the N is possible but not recommended.

**ACCESS**   From Huaraz to the village of Caraz (PT) then by hired vehicle to the power station at the outflow from Lag. Paron (4185m). Walk along N shore of lake, rough in places, then continue up the valley on N side of stream to camp by the much smaller Artesoncocha (Lag. Paron Chico) (4300m). 3h.

**CLIMB**   The normal route is on the SE-E slopes. From the camp climb NW on scree and moraine to the foot of the glacier coming down between the W and E peaks. Campsites. 3h. Climb the RHS of the glacier and then choose a route through the ice fall to reach the plateau between the peaks at 5700m. Climb the E slopes then steep snow to the airy summit, 6h.

**OTHER ROUTES**   The **S face** has some very difficult lines on ice to 70° and rock to grade V and A3.

**OTHER PEAKS**   The neighbouring peak, **Caraz Este 6020m, AD** can be climbed from the plateau by the central ice runnel in the S face (60°).

**BEST MAP**   As for Santa Cruz. Sheet 19-h 'Carhuas' is useful for the approaches.

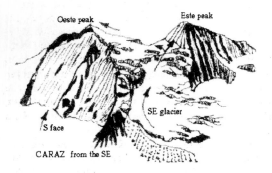

CARAZ  from the SE

ARTESONRAJU  SE face normal

# ARTESONRAJU  6025m        Map 14              5 days  AD/D

A steep snow pyramid. The most commonly climbed routes are the steep and snowy SE face from the Paron valley and the mixed N ridge from the Q. Santa Cruz. The height according to the PIGM map is only 5999m.

**ACCESS**   As for Caraz to Artesoncocha then up the obvious moraine crest to gain the glacier. Cross this easily to a high camp at 5200m S of Artesonraju from which Artesonraju, Piramide and Paron Grande can all be climbed.

**CLIMB  SE face D**. From the high camp on the Paron glacier at 5200m skirt triangular  rock area and serac zones to the R to gain the bottom of the face via the bergschrund (60°). Climb the 45-55° snow face usually best towards the LHS. Anchors often in situ, 7h.

**OTHER ROUTES**  The popular N ridge by the NE spur, **AD+** can be climbed from near Taullicocha in the Q. Santa Cruz. Approach up moraines on the RHS of the Q. Artizon then up the RHS of the glacier. The step high on the ridge should be passed on the L.

**OTHER PEAKS** The beautiful fluted peak of **Piramide de Garcilaso 5885m**  can be climbed from the 5200m camp by its 500m NW face. There are many lines on the flutings, all more or less 50-55°. **Paron Grande, 5600m, PD** can also be climbed from here by its S ridge from the S col. Finish up the W face.

**BEST MAP**   As Caraz Oeste.


# No. HUANDOY Norte  6395m          Map 15     7 days  AD/D

A beautiful massif of three main summits (N, S and W) rising like the points of a crown from the glacier filled basin (5800m) between them. The safest line to the highest peak, Huandoy Norte, is the NE face route. The easiest route is by the E icefall and central basin, but this suffers severe stonefall. The S and W peaks are normally climbed via the E icefall and central basin. For details of more difficult routes on all the Huandoy peaks see Sharman. The native name is Tullparaju.

**ACCESS**  From  Huaraz drive past the Llanganuco lakes to a bend where the road turns to the S about 2km beyond the second lake. Buses run from Yungay to Yanama and Pomabamba along this route. Descend  back to the main valley and the Pisco base camp at the entrance to the Q. Demanda. 10min. Donkeys can usually be hired here but it is better to arrange in advance from Huaraz to be sure. Cross to the N side of the river and follow sign posts to gain a path rising steeply up the hill L of the stream coming down between Huandoy and Pisco. The path is easy to follow. It goes over a flatter area, up a moraine crest, moves R, climbs  two substantial rises, passing  L of a rock outcrop on the second, to a  camp  at 4600m beneath a huge moraine (100m high). 4h. This camp is also used for Pisco.

**CLIMBS**  The highest peak, Huandoy Norte can be climbed most safely by the **NE face, D.** Traverse under Huandoy Este and climb the snow couloir to the LH of two cols, 400m, 50-70°. 8h. Camp on the plateau below the N side of the ridge. Climb either the NE ridge or face 500m, 50°. The band of loose rock at the top can be climbed in the centre, III. Then easy snow to the summit, 1-2d.

**E icefall, AD+** From the 4600m camp gain the icefall either directly or by circling under Huandoy Este. Climb the couloir at the N end of the cliff, 200m, 45°  (severe stonefall) to reach the basin. 8-10h. Good campsites. To climb Huandoy Norte from the basin skirt seracs to the W and then climb a couloir in SW flank to summit. 5h.

Huandoy Norte can also be climbed from the Paron valley to the N in several days by the **NW slopes, D**. 600m of 50° ice leads to the saddle with the W peak

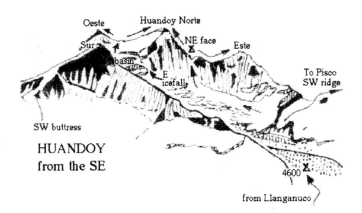

HUANDOY
from the SE

**OTHER PEAKS**  From the basin the second highest peak **Huandoy Oeste 6356m, AD** can be climbed by the E slopes and knife edge NE ridge in 5h. **Huandoy Sur, 6160m, AD** can be climbed by the fairly easy NW slopes in 5h. Huandoy Sur has some desperate ED routes up the overhanging S face. Huandoy Sur can also be climbed from Llanganuco by the SW buttress.
The outlying summit **Huandoy Este 5900, D** is easiest by the W ridge gained by climbing the 400m couloir  as for the NE face route on Huandoy Norte, then traverse the W ridge.
**BEST MAP**  Alpenvereinskarte sheet 0/3a 'Cordillera Blanca Nord' 1:100,000 or PIGM sheet 19-h 'Carhuas' 1:100,000.

## No. PISCO Oeste  5752m           Map 15               3 days  PD

One of the easiest and  most frequently climbed  peaks in the Cord. Blanca. There are however some potentially serious crevasse crossings on the SW ridge. Pisco is the Peruvian liquor, large quantities of which were drunk after the first ascent in 1951.
**ACCESS**  Follow the access for Huandoy to the camp at 4600m beneath the huge moraine. Pisco can be climbed from here but most parties camp higher. Climb the huge moraine and descend the very loose inside wall. Cross a boulder covered glacier heading generally L and pass above one circular lagoon (marked on PIGM map) to camp at a higher, smaller lagoon (4900m) (not seen until there). 4h.
**CLIMB**  Climb directly over  rock slabs then directly up the glacier to the col (5350m). Turn R at the col  and climb the N side of the broad SW ridge, usually one or two large crevasses.
**OTHER ROUTES**  The normal route can also be joined at the col by coming up from the N (Lag. Paron). There are a number of steep ice routes on the fluted S face. The easiest is a fairly direct route exiting just L of the summit, AD/D.
**OTHER PEAKS**  Another good easy peak is the small peak seen at the end from low in the Llanganuco valley. This is **Yanapaccha 5460m, PD** and can be climbed in 2d. Approach up the Q. Demanda  then walk up by the river descending from the Yanapaccha W glacier. Climb the glacier to reach the basin below the W side of the summit. Reach the ridge by a couloir (40-45°) and continue to the summit.
**BEST MAP**  As for Huandoy above.

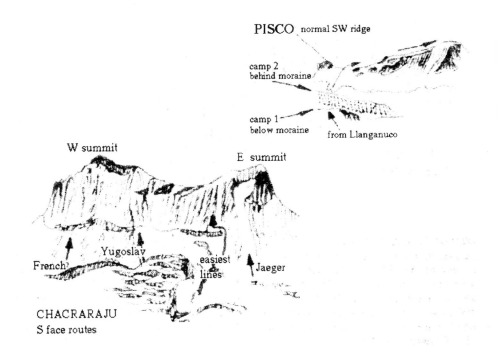

PISCO  normal SW ridge

camp 2
behind moraine

camp 1
below moraine     from Llanganuco

W summit

E summit

French?     Yugoslav     easiest
                         lines     Jaeger

CHACRARAJU
S face routes

# CHACRARAJU Oeste  6113m          Map 15          7 days  ED

Probably the hardest 6000'er in the Cord. Blanca and even in the whole of the Andes. Chacraraju is a narrow and steep sided ridge with summits at either end. The W summit is higher. Chacraraju is most often climbed by the S face though routes from the N may be slightly easier. Few parties reach the true summit of this difficult ridge. The name is Quechua and comes from the resemblance of the snow flutings to a field, 'Chakra'. Also known as Mataraju, 'twin mountain'.

**ACCESS**  From Pisco base camp follow the E side of the Q. Demanda up to the NE, then the side stream up to the simple hut at Lag. 69 (4550m). This lake is one of many not marked on the Alpenvereinskarte, but is marked on the Diaz and PIGM maps. 3h.

**CLIMB**  The easiest routes to the main summit appear to be the French direct or neighbouring routes to the R. Refer to Sharman for more details. Taking 2-3d. and with snow and ice to 90° and hanging bivouacs these are obviously very serious routes.

**OTHER ROUTES**  The first ascent climbed the NE face from Q. Huaripampa to the col between the summits then seiged the very difficult E ridge. 3-4d. To climb **Chacraraju Este, 6001, ED**, the best lines reach the ridge slightly L of the summit, 2-3d, 90°

**BEST MAP**  Alpenvereinskarte sheet 0/3a 'Cordillera Blanca Nord' 1:100,000 or PIGM sheet 18-h 'Corongo' 1:100,000. Sheet 19-h 'Carhuas' is useful for the approaches.

# No. HUASCARAN SUR 6768m    Map 15    6 days  PD
# No. HUASCARAN NORTE 6655m Map 15    6 days  PD

The massive peaks of Huascaran dominate the Cord. Blanca. The S peak is the highest mountain in Peru and curiously enough one of the easiest 6000'ers in Peru. The difficulties are normally in passing through the large ice fall to reach the col, known as the Garganta (5980m), which separates the two peaks. These difficulties vary widely from year to year depending on the number and size of the crevasses. Both peaks are relatively easy ascents from a high camp in the Garganta.

In 1970 an earthquake triggered a huge fall of ice from the N peak, which rapidly melted and formed a devastating mudslide that wiped out the town of Yungay. All but a few people in the town of 18,000 inhabitants died. The quake caused devastation in the entire Callejón de Huaylas. The native name for the peak is Matararaju.

**ACCESS**    For the normal routes the start point is the village of Musho. Musho can be reached from Huaraz by public transport via the village of Mancos. By car 2h from Huaraz. Musho has a couple of small shops and a cafe. Donkeys can be obtained very easily for the one day walk up to base camp (4150m). The route is fairly direct to the base camp which lies below and slightly L of the ice tongue coming down from the Garganta. The route starts through fields, enters a large eucalyptus plantation and then zigzags on a good path up a moraine above.

**GARGANTA CLIMB**    From the base camp go up the short rock groove on the RHS of the stream and then follow the cairns up and R over the slabs (several variations) to reach a larger stream and possible camp (4450m). Some sections to II but never exposed. From here the route goes on over glaciated slabs directly towards the S peak to gain the glacier at the highest slabs immediately R of the lowest glacier tongue (4750m - camps possible but foul). Go up over the easy angled glacier heading for the RHS of the big icefall (camps at 5250m). Follow a route through the icefall up a ramp R of the big cliff and directly under the mitre shaped snowfield (ice to 45° in some years). There is usually a very big crevasse at the top of the icefall. Once this is crossed go L (northwards) and rise gradually to reach the Garganta. Some serac danger on this last section. The usual high camp is under an ice wall at about 5900m below the W side of the Garganta - great sunsets.

The route to the Garganta used to go up the LHS of the icefall and if conditions change this may become the normal way again.

**NORTH PEAK**    From the camp gain the Garganta proper by crossing or turning several large crevasses. Gain the shoulder on the S ridge from the Garganta, avoiding crevasses as necessary. Follow the ridge to the summit (30-40°).

**SOUTH PEAK**    Gain the Garganta proper and go NE across this to a steep snow slope that leads up towards some big seracs. Climb this slope (40°) and cross the crevasse above usually by making a long traverse R (but sometimes taken directly and sometimes impassable). Go on up more or less direct over easier slopes to the summit.

**OTHER ROUTES NORTH PEAK**    There are some very impressive routes on the N face of Huascaran Norte all at ED or above. The most famous and frequently climbed appear to be the **Paragot route, ED1** up the RHS of face (60-80°, V+, 1600m) and the **NE ridge ED1** gained from NW side (60°, mostly on ice but with some rock, III-V). Both routes will need 3-4 days. See Sharman's guide for information.

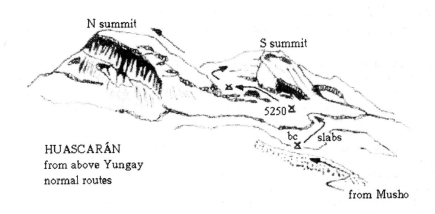

N summit

S summit

5250

bc    slabs

HUASCARÁN
from above Yungay
normal routes

from Musho

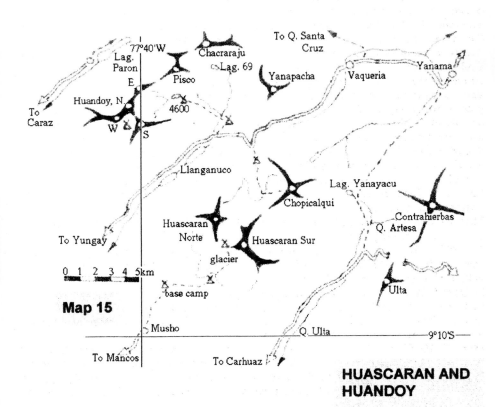

77°40'W

To Q. Santa
Cruz

Lag.
Paron          Chacraraju
                    Lag. 69
E              Pisco        Yanapacha        Vaqueria          Yanama

Huandoy, N.
                    4600
To
Caraz          W         S

Llanganuco

Lag. Yanayacu

Chopicalqui

Contrahierbas
Q. Artesa

Huascaran
Norte          Huascaran Sur

To Yungay

0 1 2 3 4 5km

glacier

Ulta

Map 15

base camp

To Mancos

Musho              Q. Ulta              9°10'S

To Carhuaz

**HUASCARAN AND
HUANDOY**

HUASCARÁN NORTE
and Garganta camp from above icefall

Normal route by S ridge

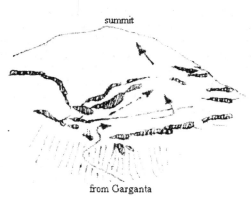

from Garganta

HUASCARAN SUR   normal route   NW face

**OTHER ROUTES SOUTH PEAK**  The **W face, D+** can be climbed from the Garganta camp. The line follows the LHS of the prominent mitre shaped snowfield (50-60°) above the ice fall, joining the poorly defined W ridge high up. 10h. The Garganta can also be reached from the E by the **E icefall**, grade n/k. There are a large number of hard TD and ED lines on the NE and E faces of Huascaran Sur. The SE ridge from the Q. Matara is also TD.

**BEST MAP**  Alpenvereinskarte sheet 0/3a 'Cordillera Blanca Nord' 1:100,000 or PIGM sheet 1:100,000. Alpenvereins also publish a 1:25,000 sheet titled 'Nevado Huascaran' but this is really just larger and blanker than the 1:100,000 sheet!

# No. CHOPICALQUI 6356m        Map 15        4 days   AD

Though dwarfed by the neighbouring Huascarán, Chopicalqui is actually one of the highest peaks in the Cord. Blanca. Climbed relatively frequently by the normal route on the SW ridge. Good views of the E faces of the Huascaran peaks.

**ACCESS**  From Huaraz via Yungay and the Llanganuco lakes to the big hairpin bend at c.4200m (PT). Walk up through trees to a meadow (4300m) where the normal base camp is situated. ½h.

**CLIMB  SW Ridge, AD.**  Gain the moraine on the W side of the meadow as soon as possible and follow the crest until cairns lead across the rubble covered glacier to the foot of the steep moraine on the far side. This moraine rises southwards from the inside corner of the junction of the glaciers coming from Chopicalqui and Huascarán. Climb the crest on a good path then loose boulders to camps at the edge of the glacier (4900m), 5h. Go up the glacier above just L of the rock rib then start to move L under big (and loose) rock wall, bypassing several big crevasses, cross the basin (poss. camps) then climb steeper slope to normal site of high camp (5600m), 5h. From here find a route around some big crevasses to gain the ridge proper. Cross a big crevasse on the extreme L and pass seracs on the L then follow the narrow and exposed ridge to summit.

**OTHER ROUTES**   The **NW ridge, TD** can be climbed from the normal base camp. Climb ESE over grass and slabs to gain the glacier. Climb via a rocky peak to the foot of the NW ridge, 6h. Climb to the col then the 60° wall and serac to gain the ridge. Climb on the S side of ridge to Chopicalqui N (6050m) then abseil to ridge beyond. Climb this on NE side to summit (55°), 2-3d. There are also several hard routes on the NW and W faces. The E and SE ridges have both been climbed from the Q. Ulta at about TD with bad cornices and snow mushrooms.

**BEST MAP**  Alpenvereinskarte sheet 0/3a 'Cordillera Blanca Nord' 1:100,000 or PIGM  sheet 19-h 'Carhuas' 1:100,000.

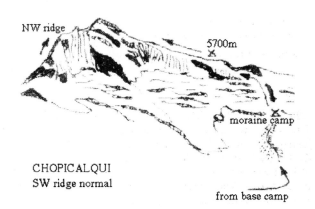

NW ridge

5700m

moraine camp

CHOPICALQUI
SW ridge normal

from base camp

# No. CONTRAHIERBAS 6036m     Map 15     5 days N/K

An extensive mountain which is rarely visited. Not a very difficult climb but bad crevasses can make an ascent time consuming. The native name is Ruricocha 'corner lake'.

**ACCESS**   From Huaraz via Carhuaz then up the Q. Ulta on the road to Chacas. From the point where the road starts to climb out the E side of the valley (4000m) (PT) continue up the main valley on foot for 2-3km to the Q. Artesa and follow this valley E to Lag. Artesa (4400m), 1d.

**CLIMB**   From Lag. Artesa climb steep slopes NE (L of prominent crag) to gain the NW ridge just R of point 5490 (5350m - camp possible). Descend the other side to the NW glacier and climb easily to the summit. 2d.

**OTHER ROUTES**   The NW glacier can also be gained from the village of Yanama and the upper reaches of Q. Ichik Ulta

**OTHER PEAKS**   On the S side of the road is the steep mixed peak, **Ulta 5875m**, a difficult climb from the Q. Ulta by either NW or NE faces.

**BEST MAP**   Alpenvereinskarte sheet 0/3a 'Cordillera Blanca Nord' 1:100,000 or PIGM sheet 19-i 'Huari' 1:100,000. Sheet 19-h 'Carhuas' is useful for the approaches.

# No. HUALCAN   6125m          Map 16               3 days  N/K

Between them Hualcan and Copa form a vast high plateau, reported to be the best place in the Cordillera Blanca for ski-mountaineering. Deep snow and long marches above 5500m can make these peaks difficult on foot.

**ACCESS**  From Huaraz to the abandoned hot spring at Hualcan (3100m). Go up the Q. Hualcan to reach Lag. Cochca (4550m) under the SW slopes of the mountain. 5h.

**CLIMB**  The normal route is the snowy S ridge gained from the W glacier about 1km N of point 5850. The summit is usually climbed with a high camp on the glacier plateau at c.5200m. Grade n/k but not too difficult.

**OTHER ROUTES**  The SW ridge can be climbed directly from the same glacier camp. Go up LHS of glacier then 50° snow face R of a mixed section. Go L of seracs to gain SW ridge. Follow this with some further difficulties, 60°, 1d.

**BEST MAP**  Alpenvereinskarte sheet 0/3a 'Cordillera Blanca Nord' or sheet 0/3b 'Cordillera Blanca Süd' 1:100,000 or PIGM sheet 19-h 'Carhuas' 1:100,000

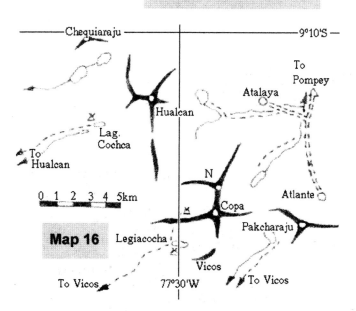

COPA AND HUALCAN

# No. de COPA 6188m      Map 16      3 days PD+

Copa is one of the easier 6000m peaks in the Cord. Blanca, but can still be harder than Huascaran. Named after a local style of hat.

**ACCESS**   From Huaraz via Marcará to the village of Vicos (PT) (3100m). From here walk slightly E of N through fields and forestry to reach distinct moraines flanking the river coming from Legiacocha. A good trail climbs the steep hillside R of this river in numerous zigzags. Finally traverse L towards Lag. Legiacocha, a beautiful blue green lake which makes a good base camp (4700m). 7h from Vicos. The W slopes of Copa can also be gained and climbed from Hac. Copa, though the lower section of glacier is apparently very badly crevassed making it difficult to find a way through.

**CLIMB**    From Legiacocha climb towards and go up the snow couloir (which lies N of the W end of the lake) to gain the summit plateau at about 5200m. The couloir reaches about 45° and is an avalanche path. From the summit plateau (camps possible) go E and negotiate sometimes serious (sometimes impassable) crevasses to reach the summit. 9h from Legiacocha.

**OTHER PEAKS**   The **N peak 6173m, PD+** is usually less severely crevassed. To climb this make a rising traverse of the glacier plateau from the top of the couloir to a point roughly due W of the summit. Then go straight to summit bypassing a few crevasses.

The short snow ridge SE of Legiacocha called **Vicos, 5325m, F** makes a good short day or acclimatisation ascent. The ridge can be traversed in either direction very easily.

**BEST MAP**   Alpenvereinskarte sheet 0/3a 'Cordillera Blanca Nord' or sheet 0/3b 'Cordillera Blanca Süd' 1:100,000 or PIGM sheet 19-i 'Huari' 1:100,000

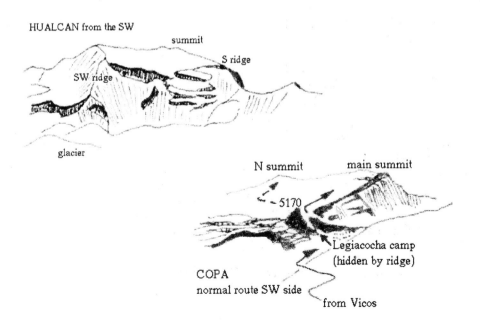

HUALCAN from the SW

summit

S ridge

SW ridge

glacier

N summit     main summit

~ 5170

Legiacocha camp
(hidden by ridge)

COPA
normal route SW side

from Vicos

**No. URUS** 5420m      Map 17      3 days   PD
**No. ISHINCA** 5530m      Map 17      3 days    F

These two easy peaks are popular acclimatisation ascents for mountaineers going on to do harder or bigger things. Both can be climbed from a camp in the upper reaches of Q. Ishinca. Urus, a chain of four peaks is shown as Yanaraju on the PIGM map. Ishinca nestles in the col between the giants Palcaraju and Ranrapalca.

**ACCESS** From Huaraz to the village of Paltay (PT) then up the track to Collon (3350m). Go through the village and take the lower trail at the fork. Cross a stream, turn R and then walk through farmland to the (usually locked) gate. Follow the track up the valley to a base camp (4300m) and refuge by the small lagoon. 8h from Collon.

**URUS CLIMB** From base camp climb the moraine crest under Urus glacier and follow it R to the glacier. Climb this until in front of a rock buttress then turn L and climb E ridge, 5h.

**ISHINCA CLIMB** Up over moraines to a high camp at the NW edge of glacier, 3h. Climb glacier towards SW ridge and climb this to the summit tower, which sometimes has a difficult bergschrund and short steep section (60°), 4h.

**OTHER ROUTES** Ishinca can also be climbed by the **NW slopes, PD** from the base camp.

**BEST MAP** As for Palcaraju

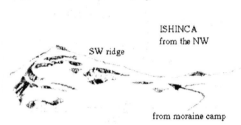

ISHINCA
from the NW

SW ridge

from moraine camp

URUS Este
from the SE

SE face

# TOCLLARAJU 6032m      Map 17      5 days   AD/D

A fairly popular peak which is usually climbed from the Q. Ishinca but can also be climbed from the Q. Aquilpo to the N. The NW ridge is easier but the W-SW face is more often successful. The name means trap mountain.

**ACCESS** As for Urus and Ishinca to the Ishinca base camp (4300m), 1d. From Ishinca base camp follow the valley E then turn N up a steep moraine crest to gain the glacier R of cliffs. Climb easy glacier slopes to a camp at 5300m, 4h. The same camp can be gained from Q. Aquilpo to the N.

**CLIMB** There are two normal routes from the 5300m camp. **W-SW face D-.** From the camp traverse R under W face and climb a line at the S end of this which gains the S ridge 100m from the summit. Pass the upper serac barrier on the R, 6h. **NW ridge, AD.** From the 5300m camp climb up and L skirting seracs to reach the shallow col above. Climb easy slopes, then cross two bergschrunds (65° - sometimes impossible) then continue to the summit, 5-6h. The NW ridge can also be climbed more directly from a camp at the NW col (5250m).

**BEST MAP** As for Palcaraju

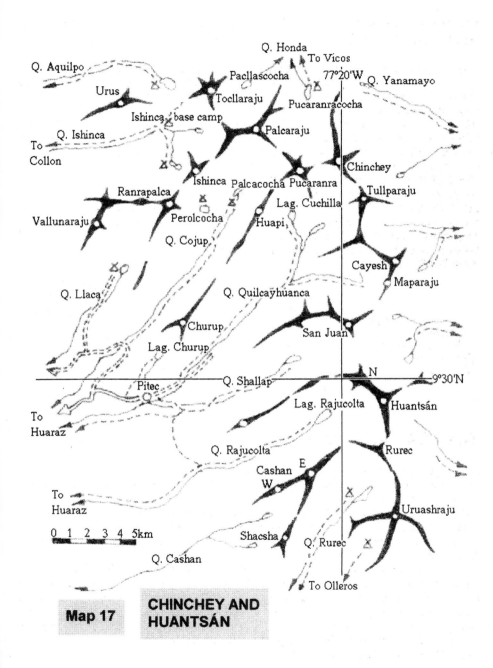

Map 17    CHINCHEY AND HUANTSÁN

TOCLLARAJU
SW face

# PALCARAJU 6274m    Map 17    6 days  N/K

The summit is a long E-W ridge with the highest point at the E end. The normal route is up the N
slopes from Q. Honda. Palcaraju means branching mountain. The mountain is also known as
Cuchilla.

**ACCESS**  From Huaraz to the village of Vicos (PT) (3100m) at the entrance to the Q. Honda. A
track goes half way up this valley to Rinconada, this can be driven but if you need donkeys
beyond Rinconada these have to be found in Vicos, probably the day before. The main trail is on
the N then E side of the river  and leads to Pucaranracocha. Before reaching this large lake climb
up the steep W slopes of the valley by a small stream to reach Pacllascocha (4600m), 7h from
Rinconada.

**CLIMB  N slopes.** From Pacllascocha ascend the NW glacier between Palcaraju and Tocllaraju
then climb the N side of the NW ridge. Traverse L across the N slopes to gain the NE ridge (50m.
of steep ice), 1d. Grade n/k.

**OTHER ROUTES**  The SW face can be climbed from Q. Cojup but the route is exposed to
considerable avalanche danger.

**BEST MAP**  Alpenvereinskarte sheet 0/3b 'Cordillera Blanca Süd' 1:100,000 or PIGM sheet
19-i 'Huari' 1:100,000

# No. RANRAPALCA 6162m   Map 17    6 days    D

The normal routes are on the NE ridge or adjacent slopes from the col with Ishinca (5350m).
This col can be gained from either Q. Ishinca to the N or Q. Cojup to the S. There are a large
number of harder routes on this popular and accessible peak.

**ACCESS**  To approach up Q. Ishinca follow the description under Ishinca and climb to the col,
2d. To approach via the  Q. Cojup hire a truck in Huaraz to take you to the valley entrance at
3950m. Walk up the valley on a good trail, first on the S side then on the N side to Lag.
Palcacocha, 14h. Just before you get to Palcacocha climb up the grassy NW slopes to reach a
large meadow. Bear L and walk directly towards Ranrapalca to reach Lag. Perolcocha (4900m).
4h. Two smaller, higher lakes can also be used as camps. The col lies a few hundred metres
above Perolcocha up moraines and scree slopes.

**CLIMB** For the **NE ridge, D** climb the steep rocky ridge from the col to the summit snowfields (6000m) then traverse S to the knife edge summit. A variation known as the **NE slopes, D**-climbs easy snow on the L of the ridge then rejoins the ridge by climbing through seracs (60°) over a bergschrund then up a 55° wall (ice, mixed or rock) L of another serac.

**OTHER ROUTES** The **SE ridge, TD+** starting just S of Perolcocha has been climbed on 65-70° snow and ice mostly on the LHS but turning many obstacles on the RHS, 2d. The beautiful **SW ridge,** seen clearly from Huaraz has also been climbed from Q. Llaca. Gain this at c.5350m by the SW face and avoid difficulties higher up by climbing a rib on the SE face, 2d.

**OTHER PEAKS** The twin summits of **Vallunaraju 5686m, PD** one of the most prominent peaks seen from Huaraz makes a good acclimatisation peak. Climb by the SW slopes from the hut in Q. Llaca (4400m) in about 8h. Between Vallunaraju and Ranrapalca is the steep sided **Ocshapalca 5881m**, a long ridge which has a number of hard gully lines on its S face.

**BEST MAP** As for Palcaraju

# No. PUCARANRA 6147m     Map 17     6 days AD+

The normal route is up the SE ridge from Lag. Cuchilla above the Q. Quilcayhuanca. Puca means red, Ranra means stony ground.

**ACCESS** Follow the access for Chinchey up the Q. Quilcayhuanca but climb the zig-zags on the LHS of the stream descending from Lag. Cuchilla to reach pleasant campsites in meadows by the lake (4600m), 2d.

**CLIMB   SE ridge AD+.** Climb moraine on the RHS of lake and turn a small crag on the R to reach the glacier. Follow ramps L through seracs to gain a flatter area immediately below a shallow col in the SE ridge (c.5700m - camps possible). Climb the ridge above passing a couple of easy rock bands, 10h from Lag. Cuchilla.

**OTHER ROUTES** The **SE face, AD+** has been climbed from just below the Pucaranra - Chinchey col (see Chinchey). Before reaching the col climb 50-55° slopes to the S of the E ridge avoiding mixed ground at the top. The **NW ridge, TD** has been climbed from Palcacocha at the head of the Cojup valley.

**BEST MAP**   As for Palcaraju.

# No. CHINCHEY 6222m        Map 17              6 days   AD

The highest peak of the extensive Chinchey massif. The most popular route is the W ridge, most easily reached from  Q. Quilcayhuanca to the S. Chinchey means puma. The peak is given a height of 6309m on the PIGM map.

**ACCESS** From Huaraz via the village of Pitec (3800m) (2h. drive) and up the Q. Quilcayhuanca. Camps can be made at the junction of Q. Cayesh (4050m), 9h, but to climb Chinchey it is better to climb higher. Continue up the valley to Tullpacocha then  climb up the RHS of the stream towards Lag. Cuchilla. Halfway up turn R through trees and follow cairns up moraines to reach a small lake (5100m) at the edge of the glacier. 2d from Huaraz.

The W ridge route can also be gained from Lag. Pucaranracocha at the head of the Q. Honda to the N. 2d from Huaraz to Pucaranracocha.

**CLIMB   W ridge, AD**. From the camp by the lake at 5100m climb the W side of the relatively flat glacier (stonefall) towards the Chinchey - Pucaranra col, 4h. Climb the crevassed 30° slopes on or just S of the ridge to reach the short 55° summit pyramid, 6h.

**OTHER ROUTES** The harder **N ridge** has been climbed from the Pucaranra col by climbing the W slopes to reach the shoulder at c.5850m.

**OTHER PEAKS**   For the keen alpinist the incredible needle of **Cayesh 5721m, TD** 7km S of Chinchey has been climbed by at least 5 hard  routes on the W face. Further S and reached from the col at the head of Q. Cayesh is the small easy peak of **Maparaju 5325m F,** climbed by its SW ridge.

**BEST MAP**   As for Palcaraju.

summit lies behind

HUAPI
from lower
Q. Cojup

W ridge

CHINCHEY
from the S

# No. HUAPI 5425m              Map 17              3 days     F

An easy  peak lying close to Huaraz which makes a good acclimatisation  ascent. Great views of the Chinchey group from the summit. The peak is also known as Jatunmontepuncu, the great doorway mountain.

**ACCESS**   From Huaraz straight up hill to the Q. Cojup entrance at 3950m. (hire a truck!). Walk in along the relatively flat quebrada (as for Ranrapalca) until directly below the peak.

**CLIMB**   Steeply up grass and then scree to gain the glaciated SW ridge. Follow this to summit, some large crevasses.

**BEST MAP**   As for Palcaraju.

## No. CASHAN Este 5723m          Map 17                 6 days   PD

One of the easier peaks in the Huantsán group. Cashan means spiny.
**ACCESS**    From Huaraz to the village of Macashca (PT) then up the N side of the long Q.
Rajucolta (Pariac on PIGM maps) to Lag. Rajucolta (4300m) (also called Tambillo) 2d. The
quebrada can also be entered by crossing the broad col (4250m) SE of Pitec, without losing too
much height.
**CLIMB**    From the huts below Lag. Rajucolta follow the path S up the steep Q. Pumahuanca.
Turn R and follow cairns over moraines then slabs to the glacier. Climb this and then the R
sloping ramp to reach the W ridge. Follow this on snow to the summit, 1d.
**BEST MAP**    As for Huantsán.


# No. HUANTSÁN 6395m          Map 17                 8 days   TD

The highest peak of the southern Cord. Blanca and after Chacraraju probably the hardest big
peak in the whole range.
**ACCESS**    As for Cashan to the Lag. Rajucolta. From here climb the small valley SE of the lake
to a meadow then climb out the L flank of this valley and pass a small rock cliff and the ruins of
a camp. Enter a small bowl and leave this by the L, following a stream which leads up to Lag.
Ahuac (4780m).
**CLIMB**    The easiest route to the summit almost traverses over **Huantsán Norte 6113m**. From
Lag. Ahuac gain the W glacier and cross this under the W face of Huantsán heading towards
Huantsán Norte. Climb the snow slopes on the RHS of the SW ridge of Huantsán Norte to gain a
col (5950m). From here the main peak of Huantsán can be reached by the difficult NNW ridge,
keeping mostly to the steep snow on the E side to avoid towers. 2-3d.
**OTHER PEAKS**    To the N of Huantsán is the relatively popular peak **San Juan 5843m, AD**
Climb by the S side of the NW ridge from the col at 5200m. Gain the col from either Q. Cayesh
to the N or Q. Shallap to the S.
**BEST MAP**    Alpenvereinskarte sheet 0/3b 'Cordillera Blanca Süd' 1:100,000 or PIGM sheet
20-i 'Recuay' 1:100,000

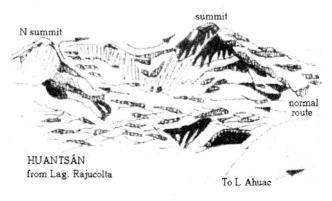

HUANTSÁN
from Lag. Rajucolta

## No. URUASHRAJU  5735m          Map 17              4 days   AD

A relatively easy snow peak with good views of Huantsán.
**ACCESS**  From Huaraz via the village of Olleros (3500m) (PT). Follow the Olleros to Chavin trail but cross the river by a bridge in a gorge before Qollotococha. Follow a path up into the Q. Pumahuacanca to the glacier edge SW of the summit, 7h.
**CLIMB  S ridge**. Cross the glacier to the col (5300m) below the narrow S ridge, and follow this up to the summit (45°), 4h.
**OTHER ROUTES** The **W ridge PD** can also be climbed from Pumahuacanca, joining the S ridge just below summit.
**OTHER PEAKS**  Near the entrance to the Q. Rurec **Shacsha 5703m, AD** can be climbed most easily by the W flank of the S ridge.
**BEST MAP**  As for Huantsán.


## No. YANAMAREY Norte  5262m      Map 18              2 days   PD
## No. YANAMAREY Sur   5220m       Map 18              2 days   F

The N and S peaks of Yanamarey are easy peaks that make good acclimatisation ascents. They can both be climbed from the Q. Yanamarey and the S peak can in fact be climbed in one day from near the Punta Cahuish tunnel on the Chavin road. The name means black pestle.
**ACCESS**  For the Q. Yanamarey drive from Huaraz via Catac to the large, beautiful lake of Querococha (3980m) (PT). Follow a path along the NW shore and up the valley to the obvious fork. The R fork leads up to good camps by lagoons (4600m) under Yanamarey Sur, the L to the S side of Yanamarey Norte. To climb both peaks a camp near the fork in the Q. Yanamarey at 4400m would make sense, 2-3h to the fork from Querococha.
**YANAMAREY NORTE CLIMB**  Yanamarey Norte can be climbed easily by the rocky S side, II, 5-6h from fork
**YANAMAREY SUR CLIMB**  From the last lagoon in the valley W of the summit climb moraines to a L sloping rock ramp then back R over slabs to gain the glacier. Go up this moving R to join the S ridge, 5-6h from fork. The S ridge can also be joined from the Punta Cahuish tunnel.
**OTHER ROUTES**  Yanamarey Norte 5262m can also be climbed from the Q. Araranca by the N glacier and icy N ridge. 3d.
**BEST MAP**  As for Huantsán.

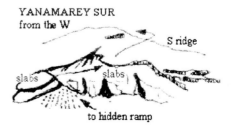

YANAMAREY SUR
from the W

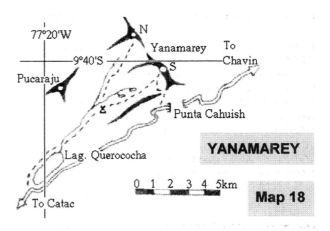

| No. RARIA Norte 5590m | Map 19 | 3 days N/K |
|---|---|---|
| **No. RARIA** Sur  5530m | Map 19 | 3 days N/K |

The two main peaks of the Raria massif, Raria Norte and Raria Sur can be combined from a camp in the Q. Huaiyacu. This is a good area for a preliminary acclimatisation trip.

**ACCESS**   From Huaraz via Pachacoto and up the Rio Pumapampa towards Pastoruri (plenty tourist buses go this way). Get out 4km before Pastoruri almost opposite the track up to the Mina San Anton and go down to the river (back track slightly). Walk NE up the Q. Huaiyacu to a camp by the Lag. Verdecocha (4600m) at the foot of the Raria peaks. 1d.

**RARIA NORTE**   Ascend the SE glacier of the massif to the col between the peaks (5200m). Descend to the base of the S slopes and climb these on snow and ice. Not difficult, 1d. The peak can also be climbed from the Q. Raria to the N.

**RARIA SUR**   Can be climbed from the col by the rocky NE ridge.

**OTHER PEAKS**   The other Raria peaks are relatively easy. Also easy are most summits in the **Pongos** massif to the N. The latter are not detailed here as names and routes are confused, but access is relatively easy from Catac up the Quebradas Queshque and Pamparaju to the W of the peaks.

**BEST MAP**   As for Huantsán.

## CAULLARAJU Este  5686m     Map 19     3 days  N/K
## No. TUCO  5479m           Map 19     2 days   F

The final group at the S end of the Cord. Blanca has some enjoyable and easy lower peaks. Tuco is Quechua for owl.

**ACCESS**  For both peaks access is from Huaraz via Pachacoto and up the Rio Pumapampa road towards Pastoruri (PT). **1.** For Caullaraju leave the road at Lag. Patococha just before Carpa. Approach up the Q. Huicsa valley from the road, 1d. **2.** For Tuco leave the road about 4km before the Pastoruri turn off on a track that goes up the S side of the valley to the Mina San Anton (4900m). From the mine traverse E into Q. Pastoruri. Head for the NW slopes of Tuco and camp by a small lake (4850m).

**CAULLARAJU CLIMB**  The highest peak of the complex Caullaraju massif is the E peak lying S of the head  of the Q. Huicsa. Climb either the NE face on snow or the NE ridge on rock. Neither believed to be difficult.

**TUCO CLIMB**  From the lake (4850m) climb easily up the NW glacier. 1d. if acclimatised.

**BEST MAP**  As for Huantsán.

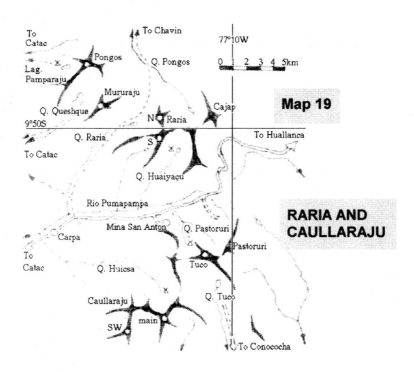

Photo: **Huascaran Norte from the camp at 5250m, Cordillera Blanca, Peru**. J. Biggar.

To Huaraz

Chiquian

Huayhuash

Yerupajé

HUANUCO

To Trujillo

Cajatambo

Raura

Huagaruncho

Huachon

Oyon

CERRO DE PASCO

Lago Junin

Ondores

Huacho

Canta

Sta Ana

La Viuda

Morococha

LA OROYA

Jallacate

Chosica

Matucana

Central

12°S

LIMA

**Map 20**

0   25    50    75km

Miraflores

HUANCAYO

Huarochiri

Yauyos

Pacific
Ocean

77°W

Cañete

To Ica

**CENTRAL PERUVIAN
CORDILLERAS**

Photo:  **Hot springs at Upis beneath the North face of Ausangate, Cordillera Vilcanota,
Peru.** J. Biggar.

# CHIQUIAN   Access town for the Cord. Huayhuash          3041m

The small town of Chiquian has become famous as the entry point to the spectacular Cordillera Huayhuash. A world famous trek starts and finishes in the town, taking in a complete circuit of the Huayhuash mountains in ten to twelve days.

To reach Chiquian turn off the main Lima to Huaraz road at Conococha. About 7h travel from Lima to Chiquian. There are direct buses from Lima but it may be easier to go via Huaraz. There are several buses a day from Huaraz to Chiquian, about 2h. From the road at Conococha there are great views of the Huayhuash. Facilities in Chiquian are a bit limited, but there are simple hotels and restaurants and it is easy to obtain pack animals for the long base camp approaches because of the popularity of the trek.

**FOOD**   Several small grocery stores round the centre of town, but there is a much better choice in Huaraz (or even Lima).

**FUEL**   Kerosene from shops in town. If you need Camping Gas better to buy it in Huaraz.

**MOUNTAIN INFO AND EQUIPMENT**   Best sources are in Huaraz but in Chiquian try Sport Yerupajá.


# JIRISHANCA 6094m          Map 21          9 days   D/TD

At the N end of the range, Jirishanca is one of the most dramatic and difficult peaks in the Huayhuash and one of the hardest 6000'ers in the Andes. The name means 'peak of the humming bird'.

**ACCESS**   As for Yerupajá from Chiquian to Solteracocha and on to the glacier. Once on the Yerupajá glacier traverse L at c.5200m to a corridor between the W face of Yerupajá Chico and a minor peak (5545m). Descend to the base of the SW face of Jirishanca. (5100m), 3d from Chiquian.

**CLIMB**   Start R of the central rocky face. Climb mixed or ice slopes to pass some seracs (65°). Continue up skirting a second serac zone to the R and climb flutings towards the W ridge. On the ridge climb loose mixed ground to reach the summit crest and follow this S to the summit.

**OTHER ROUTES**   The Cassin route gains the W ridge much lower on the mountain by mixed ground (70°, IV+).

**OTHER PEAKS**   To the N lies **Rondoy 5870m, ED+** a very serious and difficult ascent by the W face to the col between the N and S summits. Further N is the more practicable **Ninashanca 5637m, D** which can be climbed from Lag. Mitucocha by the NE ridge, gained by a 45° snow couloir then a short rock pitch (III) followed by the corniced ridge.

**BEST MAP**   As for Yerupajá.

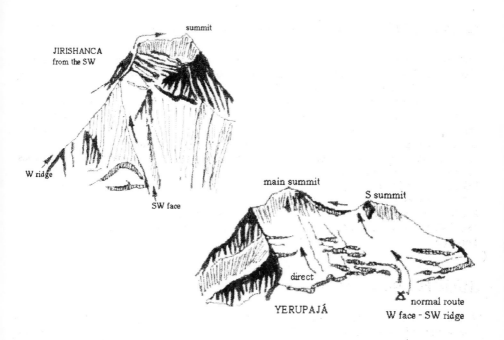

JIRISHANCA
from the SW

summit

W ridge

SW face

main summit

S summit

direct

normal route
W face - SW ridge

YERUPAJÁ

# No. YERUPAJÁ 6634m·     Map 21     9 days     D

Yerupajá, the highest peak in the Huayhuash is a spectacular wedge of snow and ice. It is the third highest peak in Peru after the Huascarán summits, but is considerably more difficult and much less busy. The normal route is by the SW ridge, gained from the W.

**ACCESS**   From Chiquian descend to the Rio Quero then climb up the Rio Llamac valley to the village of Llamac (3300m). From here head SE over the high pass known as Pampa Llamac (4300m) to reach the Q. Pacllon valley coming down from Lag. Jahuacocha and Lag. Solteracocha. The lakes make a good low base camp (4100m), 2d. Go along the S side of Solteracocha on a steep path then climb the W side of the Yerupajá glacier on two moraines separated by rock ledges. Gain the glacier and go up to a high camp at c.5500m between Yerupajá and Rasac, 1d.

**CLIMB**   Climb the snow slope (55°) to the L of the S summit passing the lowest seracs on the R. A steeper section (60°) to the L of a small rocky pinnacle leads to the summit ridge which can be difficult if heavily corniced. 12h.

**OTHER ROUTES**   To the L of the normal route the **W face** can be climbed direct on snow slopes and ice runnels (to 65°) to reach the ridge N of the summit. If the SW ridge is difficult this route may offer an easier way to the summit. The **NE face** can be climbed with difficulty (65°/III) from Lag. Carhuacocha.

**BEST MAP**   Alpenvereinskarte sheet 0/3c 'Cordillera Huayhuash' 1:100,000 or PIGM sheet 21-j 'Yanahuanca' 1:100,000. Sheet 21-i 'Chiquian' is useful for access.

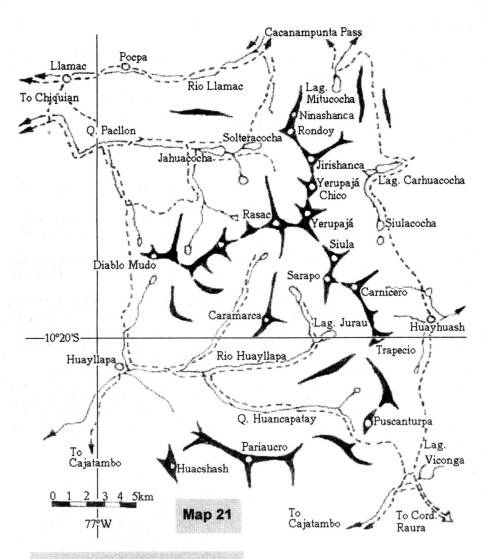

Cacanampunta Pass

Pocpa

Llamac

To Chiquian

Rio Llamac

Lag. Mitucocha

Ninashanca

Q. Pacllon

Solteracocha    Rondoy

Jahuacocha

Jirishanca

Yerupajá Chico    Lag. Carhuacocha

Rasac

Yerupajá    Siulacocha

Siula

Diablo Mudo

Sarapo

Carnicero

Caramarca

Lag. Jurau    Huayhuash

10°20'S

Rio Huayllapa    Trapecio

Huayllapa

Q. Huancapatay    Puscanturpa

To Cajatambo    Pariaucro    Lag. Viconga

Huacshash

0  1  2  3  4  5km

77°W    **Map 21**

To Cajatambo    To Cord. Raura

**CORDILLERA HUAYHUASH**

## No. RASAC   6017m                   Map 21                  8 days   AD

The easiest of the 6000m peaks in the Huayhuash, Rasac lies about 3km W of Yerupajá and is often climbed as a warm up before Yerupajá. The name Rasac is derived from the Quechua for toad.
**ACCESS**   As for Yerupajá to the camp in the glacier basin at c..5500m, 3d.
**CLIMB**   By the E face, several different lines are possible at grades from AD to D, grade II-III rock and snow or ice to 50°. Bad stonefall has been reported. 1d.
**BEST MAP**   As for Yerupajá.

## No. SIULA GRANDE   6352m            Map 21              12 days   D

A mountain which has become famous because of Joe Simpson's exploits in a crevasse after falling during descent of the normal route after completing the first ascent of the W face in 1985. The normal route is the N ridge from the Lag. Carhuacocha.
**ACCESS**   From Chiquian to Llamac (3300m) then continue on up the Rio Llamac through the village of Rondoy and over the Cacanampunta pass (4700m). Turn towards the S and Mitucocha then  SE to Lag. Carhuacocha (4138m), 4d from Chiquian.
**CLIMB**   From Carhuacocha walk up the valley to the W to reach the small lagoon under the W face of Yerupajá Chico. Climb S from here to gain the flatter upper section of the Yerupajá glacier and go up this to the Yerupajá - Siula col (5730m), camps possible. Cross the bergschrund above and climb towards the N ridge, keeping L at first. Then climb a rock or mixed pitch (III) and  continue along the narrowing crest to the summit. 3d from Carhuacocha.
**OTHER ROUTES**   Superstition may prevent anyone repeating the very difficult W face!
**OTHER PEAKS**   From the Lag. Carhuacocha base **Sarapo 6127m** can be climbed in 3-4 days by the E face. Climb S past Siulacocha and Quesillacocha to gain the badly crevassed Sarapo glacier. Climb this by the S side to reach a snow plateau (5500m) beneath the E face of Sarapo. From here climb steeply to the summit on rock, ice and mixed ground, finishing by a couloir (60-65°) between seracs.
**BEST MAP**   As for Yerupajá.

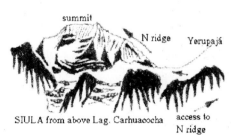

SIULA from above Lag. Carhuacocha

## PUSCANTURPA Sur 5550m                Map 21        7 days   PD

One of the easiest peaks in the Huayhuash, known also as Cuyoc or Puyoc. The peak lies just N of the Punta Cuyoc pass half way round the famous Huayhuash circuit trek and can be climbed easily from near the pass in a short day. The length of time needed to complete the climb from Chiquian would be 10-12 days - the time of 7 days is for the shortest approach from Cajatambo.
**ACCESS**   Quickest access is via the village of Cajatambo (3380m)(PT) lying SW of the Huayhuash. From here cross the steep pass to the N (4150m) to reach the Rio Pumarinri and follow this E and then N to Lag. Viconga on the Huayhuash circuit. From here climb up to the small lagoon (4900m) below the S slopes of the peak, 3d. From Chiquian follow the circuit trek counter-clockwise to Llamac then S to Huayllapa and E up the Q. Huanacpatay to the Punta Cuyoc, 4-5 d.
**CLIMB**   From the small lagoon (4900m) which lies below the S slopes  climb directly up scree slopes towards the summit. Turn the first serac on the L and  the second on the R, then continue to the summit.
**OTHER PEAKS**   The slightly higher **Puscanturpa Norte 5652m** can be climbed with greater difficulty by the rocky SW ridge, gained from the W side of Punta Cuyoc (grade VI - good rock).
**BEST MAP**   As for Yerupajá.

## LIMA   The capital of Peru, a sprawling coastal city                150m

Most people hate the dirty, smoggy sprawl of Lima, Peru's capital city. It does grow on you a little after a few weeks, but it is never a pleasant place. The city must have the world's most bizarre climate; Lima is a desert city with less than 50mm rainfall per year (drier than most of Arabia and Egypt) and a tropical city at sea level. Despite this, during the main climbing season of May - September, Lima is plagued by five months of dreadful  mist with occasional outbreaks of thin drizzle. It is cold (12-15°C) and the damp climate covers everything in grime.
**SIGHTS**   There are some museums and archaeological sites worth seeing  in and around the city. Particularly recommended are the Gold Museum and the ruins of  Pachacamac to the S of the city. Miraflores has some good beaches in the Lima summer (November - March).
**FOOD**   There are a number of big supermarkets  in the central area of Miraflores with a good choice of dried foods etc. (a much better choice than in provincial cities).
**MOUNTAIN INFO**   South American Explorers Club is a reasonable source of information on mountaineering and a very good source for travel in general. It is also a good place to contact other climbers in Lima if you're looking for a partner. Also worth trying are the Peruvian guides (AGMP) offices at Paz Soldan 225, San Isidro.

## Co. YARUPAC   5685m   Map 22   4 days  N/K
## Co. SANTA ROSA   5706m   Map 22   4 days  N/K

These are the two highest peaks of the Cord. Raura which lies SE of the Cord. Huayhuash. These mountains are much quieter than the Huayhuash mountains.

**ACCESS**   Access is easiest from the village of Oyon (3630m) (PT) to the S of the range. Shops and lodging. Buses from Lima via Huacho. From Oyon follow the valley N to Pucallpa. For Santa Rosa go NE from here to the Mina Raura (4600m) on a high plateau in the centre of the range at 4800m - about 20km. It may be possible to drive this section. For Yarupac go NW from Pucallpa past Lag. Surasaca to a base camp W of the peak (4400m). A road (condition n/k) now goes from here to Lag. Viconga in the Cord. Huayhuash and the peaks could also be gained from Cajatambo to the W.

**SANTA ROSA CLIMB**   The normal route is by the glaciated N face from the Mina Raura road, 1d. Probably about AD.

**YARUPAC CLIMB**   Climb by the W ridge, no details and grade n/k.

**OTHER PEAKS**   Near the Mina Raura is **Flor de Luto, 5529m** climbed by various routes on S side. **Cule 5580m,** also known as Kuli or Rumiwain, has been climbed by its NW ridge. **Condorsenja 5379m,** has been climbed easily from the N and NE.

**BEST MAP**   PIGM sheet 21-j 'Yanahuanca' 1:100,000. Sheet 22-j 'Oyon' useful for access.

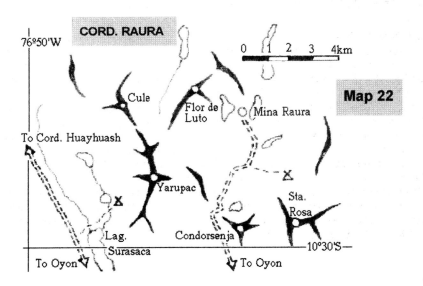

## No. RAUJUNTE   5477m          Map 23          2 days  N/K

The highest point of the Cord. La Viuda which lies inland from Lima and N of the main road and rail link to Huancayo. The mountains rise from a high rolling plateau (4400-4800m) scattered with many small lakes. These peaks can be reached easily in a day from Lima, though for acclimatisation it may be better to stay in the large town of La Oroya (c. 3400m) for a couple of days. There are tracks into most of the main valleys leading to small mines.
**ACCESS** For Raujunte approach up the Q. Chinchan, leaving the main Lima road at the large hairpin bend 3km beyond Casapalca (about 10km before Morococha). From here a track heads NW to good camping (4700m) beneath the S slopes of the peak.
**CLIMB** By W ridge. No details but easy. 1d.
**OTHER PEAKS** There are many other peaks just over the 5000m mark all with easy access. For many of the northern peaks in the range such as **Torreon 5362m** access is probably easier from Ondores in the Mantaro valley to the NE.
**BEST MAP** PIGM sheet 24-k 'Matucana' 1:100,000.

## No. TUNSHU   5730m          Map 23          5 days  N/K
## No. TICLLA   5897m          Map 23          5 days  N/K

These are the two highest peaks in the range which is generally known as the Cord. Central. This lies S of the main Lima - Huancayo road and rail link. Being close to Lima the area has been opened up to mining and access is relatively easy along the many tracks.
**TUNSHU ACCESS** From Canchayllo in the Mantaro valley to the Hac. Cochas then walk W for about 15km. Also possible from Huari in the Mantaro valley by track to the village of Huayhuay then walk S-SW to reach the E side of the mountain. About 20km. It may be possible to drive some of the other mining roads in the area, 1-2d.
**TICLLA ACCESS** For Ticlla travel from either Cañete on the coast or Huancayo inland to get to the village of Yauyos. About 20km N of Yauyos is Miraflores (3650m) from where a valley leads W to Lag. Huasacocha under the S slopes of Ticlla.
**TUNSHU CLIMB** The NE ridge, first climbed in 1958. Mixed, grade n/k, but not too difficult.
**TICLLA CLIMB** Also known as Cotoni. A difficult ascent by the W face.
**OTHER PEAKS** S of Ticlla is the steep fluted snow pyramid of **Llongote 5781m,** reported to be a very difficult climb.
**BEST MAP** The peaks lie around the junction of four PIGM sheets, 24-k, 24-l, 25-k and 25-l, all at 1:100,000.

NE ridge

TUNSHU from the E

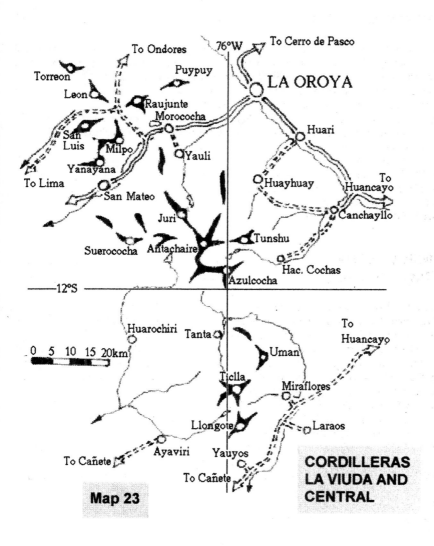

To Ondores
76°W
To Cerro de Pasco

Torreon
Puypuy
LA OROYA

Leon
Raujunte
Morococha
Huari

San
Luis
Milpo
Yauli

Yanayana
Huayhuay
To
Huancayo

To Lima
San Mateo
Canchayllo

Juri
Tunshu

Suerococha
Antachaire
Hac. Cochas

12°S
Azulcocha

Huarochiri
Tanta
To
Huancayo

0  5  10  15  20km
Uman

Ticlla
Miraflores

Llongote
Laraos

To Cañete
Ayaviri
Yauyos
**CORDILLERAS
LA VIUDA AND
CENTRAL**

**Map 23**
To Cañete

# HUAGARUNCHO  5730m       Map 24        5-7 days   N/K

A difficult and isolated peak lying  NE of  Cerro de Pasco.

**ACCESS**  From the large town of Cerro de Pasco via Huachon to Tarata, 1-2d.

**CLIMB**  The first ascent and the easiest line is by the W ridge, gained from the N. It is difficult, with poor snow and ice, big seracs and bad cornices.

**OTHER PEAKS**  150km further S lies the Cord. Huaytapallana whose highest peak **Jallacate, 5567m** can be climbed from the city of Huancayo (3300m). Access by track through Vilcacoto to 4600m on SW slopes. The peaks of the Cord. Huaytapallana are heavily glaciated but relatively easy.

**BEST MAP**  Recently published PIGM  sheets 22k and 221 at 1:100,000.

HUAGARUNCHO
W ridge

from N flank

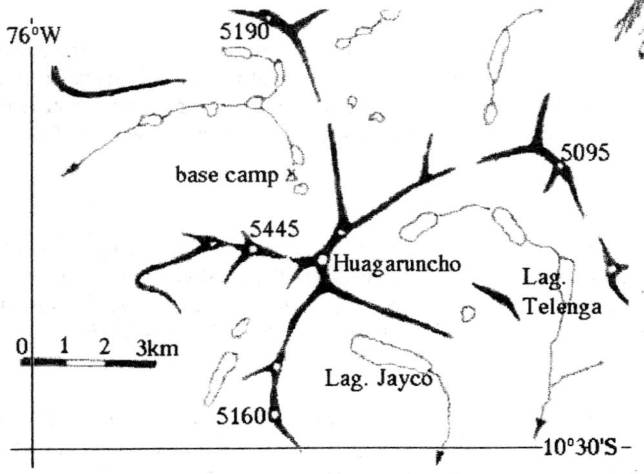

76°W    5190

base camp

5095

5445

Huagaruncho

Lag.
Telenga

0  1  2  3km

Lag. Jayco

5160

10°30'S

Map 24        HUAGARUNCHO

# SOUTHERN PERU

## INTRODUCTION
Some of the wildest and least explored ranges in the Andes lie in southern Peru in the area around Cuzco. Numerous Cordilleras and Nudos are found on the eastern edge of the Altiplano, where the high plateau meets the Amazon basin.

The peaks are all heavily glaciated and very Alpine, with some ranges rivalling the Cordillera Blanca and Huayhuash for spectacular peaks. There aren't many technically easy peaks in this part of Peru and there aren't many accessible peaks either. As a consequence it is very quiet and you will probably be the only team on your mountain even on the busiest peaks like Ausangate and Salkantay.

This chapter deals only with the main ranges around Cuzco. The Cordillera Apolobamba on the Bolivian border are in the Bolivia chapter and the high volcanic peaks around Arequipa are in the Cordillera Occidental chapter.

This is the best part of South America to visit if you want to see the real South America, with colourful highland Indians, Inca ruins, llamas and condors. The fantastic stone work of the many Inca ruins in and around Cuzco should not be missed.

## GETTING THERE
The only easy way to get to the area is by flying to Cuzco via Lima, the Peruvian capital. See under northern Peru for details of flights to Lima. There are several flights daily from Lima to Cuzco with the Peruvian airlines, Faucett, AeroPeru and Americana. The bus journey from Lima to Cuzco is a very long 33 hours, passing through areas that can be dangerous because of armed robbery etc. It is not recommended.

## SEASON
The climbing season in this part of Peru is the June to August dry season. The weather appears to be less reliable than either Bolivia to the S or the Cord. Blanca to the N. Many ranges are near to the Amazon and have relatively wet climates with afternoon storms even in the dry season. Temperatures are very cold with freezing levels about 4000m at night in the dry season.

## CLIMBING CONDITIONS
Deep new snow is common even in season and because the mountains are rarely climbed this can lead to problems. Snow lines are at about 5000m. The western and southern slopes have noticeably more snow and ice, the eastern and northern slopes generally more rock. Where there is ice it is generally very good.

The naming of peaks in the area is very confused, particularly in the Cordillera Vilcanota where even the main 6000m peaks seem to be known by several different (but unfortunately similar) sets of names. The names used in this guide for the Vilcanota are widely used in mountaineering literature (e.g.Neate) but do not always correspond to local or PIGM usage.

## OTHER GUIDE BOOKS
Backpacking in Peru and Bolivia, 6th Ed., Bradt Publications.
No climbing guides known.

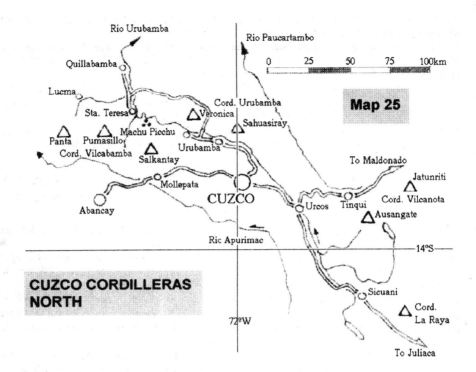

Map 25

CUZCO CORDILLERAS NORTH

# CUZCO The ancient Inca capital, now a regional centre    3310m

Cuzco (or Qosqo) was the ancient capital of the Inca Empire and in and around the city are many traces of the fabulous architecture they left behind. No-one should come to this part of South America without spending some of their time exploring the fascinating archaeology. The city of Cuzco sits in a high basin at 3310m on a plateau between the rivers Urubamba and Apurimac. For mountaineers the city makes a good base for acclimatisation and the opportunity to see some of South America's most spectacular tourist sites.

**SIGHTS**   There are so many ruins around Cuzco that no guide could list all those worth seeing but Sacsayhuaman, an incredible toothed fortress which sits on the hillside immediately N of Cuzco is probably the most spectacular. There are good views of Ausangate from here.

**MACHU PICCHU**   Set on a spectacular neck of rock almost 1000m above the deep gorge of the Urubamba river, Machu Picchu is a sight that should not be missed. Manic mountaineers can console themselves for a wasted day by ascending the steep peak which forms the classic backdrop to Machu Picchu. **Huayna Picchu, 2660m.** There is a path to the top, but several steep staircases almost merit a rock grade of I. The path round the LHS to the Temple of the Moon is even more spectacular.

The 3 day Inca Trail to Machu Picchu starting at the rail halt known as km88 is worth doing. Though quite busy it provides a great way of acclimatising, with passes up to 4200m and superb views of Salkantay and the Pumasillo group. The ruins which are seen along the way are increasingly spectacular as you walk towards Machu Picchu.

**FOOD**  Several big grocers shops near the centre of town. Try the one on the N side of Plateros.

**FUEL**  Petrol and kerosene from the petrol stations on Saphi. Camping Gas from several shops around the Plaza that also sell and rent camping equipment.

**MOUNTAIN TRANSPORT AND INFO**  There are numerous agencies in and around the Plaza de Armas who can arrange mountain transport, donkeys and or porters. Most are set up for trekkers, and particularly those doing the Inca Trail. Ask around for the best prices.

**MOUNTAIN EQUIPMENT**  There are many agencies around town renting and selling camping gear. Climbing gear is harder to find, but try 'Deportes' at Av. del Sol 346.

# PUMASILLO 6070m      Map 26          12 days N/K
# LASUNAYOC 5960m      Map 26          10 days N/K

Pumasillo is the highest point of an extensive group of difficult peaks near the W end of the remote Cordillera Vilcabamba. The name means the Puma's Claw.

**ACCESS**  From Cuzco by rail to Santa Teresa, then by mule via the Yanama pass (4770m) to the village of Yanama (3510m), S of the peak. From Yanama continue via Paccha (3900m) to reach a base camp under W ridge. About 4d.

**PUMASILLO CLIMB**  The normal route and line of first ascent is the W ridge. Avoid the prominent rock buttress low down by climbing around the N side of it on the W glacier. Move back R to the W ridge. Climb over flutings and an ice bulge then follow ridge to the summit ice formations. Difficult. 2-3d.

**LASUNAYOC CLIMB**  From the W side of the Yanama pass follow the valley N to the Lasunayoc col (5300m). Climb the E slopes and ridge with some steep ice and seracs high up.

**OTHER PEAKS**  SE of Pumasillo is the difficult ice peak **Sacsarayoc 5996m** climbed by the E ridge, gained by a long traverse from the Lasunayoc col across the N slopes of Lasunayoc.

**BEST MAP**  None available.

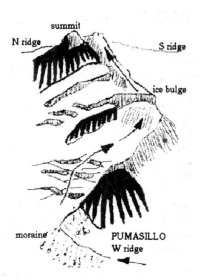

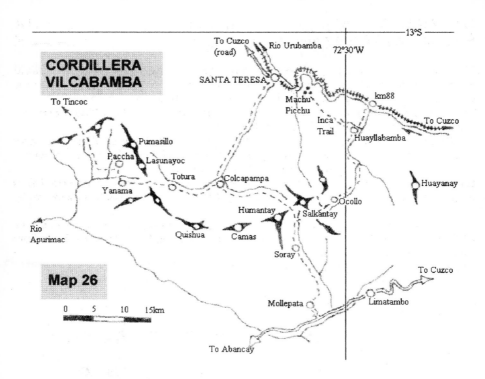

**SALKANTAY** 6271m    Map 26    8 days  AD
**HUMANTAY** 5917m    Map 26    7 days AD+

The massive Salkantay is the highest peak in the Cord. Vilcabamba. It has an impressive S face as does the neighbouring peak of Humantay.

**ACCESS** From Cuzco by bus, truck or jeep to Mollepata (2800m), then by mule through Soray (3850m), then E over the pass of Incachillasca to a small settlement. About 3d. This point can also be reached from km88 on the Machu Picchu railway by walking up the valley to the S through Huayllabamba, 2d. From the settlement a further day will be needed up the pass to the N to reach a base camp in a pleasant meadow under the NE ridge.

**SALKANTAY CLIMB** The normal route is the NE ridge from a camp below the col at c.4500m. Gain the ridge by a rising traverse of the glacier to a snow saddle or, more easily, by a rocky crest leading to the same saddle. Bivouac possible on last rocks at c.5500m. The snow/ice ridge above is followed over several short steep sections.

**HUMANTAY CLIMB** Easiest ascent is from the NE, either up a shattered rock buttress or winding up the high E facing glacier to gain the summit ridge.

**BEST MAP** None available.

## No. VERONICA   5682m          Map 25          3 days  N/K
## No. SAHUASIRAY   5720m        Map 25          5 days  N/K

These two peaks are the highest in the Urubamba range which lies N of the river of the same
name. The peaks are relatively easy to get to from Cuzco and certainly more accessible than any
others in SE Peru. The range consists of several isolated massifs known as 'nudos'.

**ACCESS**   For Veronica from Cuzco via Ollantaytambo then up to the Abra Malaga pass (PT)
on the road which leads to Santa Teresa and Quillabamba.

**VERONICA CLIMB**   Veronica is a beautiful snow pyramid clearly seen from the upper
Urubamba valley. It is also known as Huacay Huilcay, Waqaywillka or Padre Eterno. The normal
route is by the NE ridge from Abra Malaga (4350m). Grade n/k.

**SAHUASIRAY CLIMB**  Sahuasiray is a steep peak sometimes known as Chainapuerto. This is
the name given more specifically to a summit lying N of the main peak. The first ascent was by
the E ridge gained from the S. Grade n/k.

**OTHER PEAKS** The peak E of Veronica is **Helancoma 5367m,** climbed on SE side from
Ollantaytambo. The peak W of Sahuasiray is **No. Chicon (Media Luna) 5530m,** climbed from
the village of Urubamba to the SW.

**BEST MAP**   PIGM sheet 27-r 'Urubamba' 1:100,000.

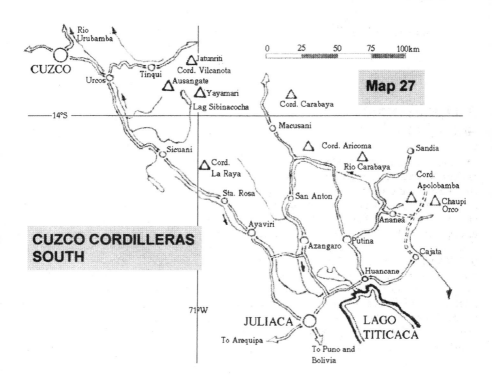

## TACUSIRI  5400m                    Map 29              5 days    F/PD

Tacusiri is the most westerly main peak in the extensive Cordillera Vilcanota. The peak is marked on the PIGM map as Tacusiri but seems to be known as Sorimani in some sources. The ascent is an easy scramble from Pucacocha with fine views of the huge icefalls on the S and W sides of Ausangate.

**ACCESS**   From Tinqui via Upis to Pucacocha. Beautiful campsite. 2d.

**CLIMB**   From Pucacocha climb onto the low ridge lying due S and scramble to the summit over rock and scree on the S side of E ridge. Grade about F or PD.

**OTHER PEAKS AND ROUTES**   Both Tacusiri and Sorimani (to the N) can probably be climbed from Pucacocha by the glacier col between them. The superb rock needle E of Sorimani has also been climbed.

**BEST MAP**   As for Ausangate.

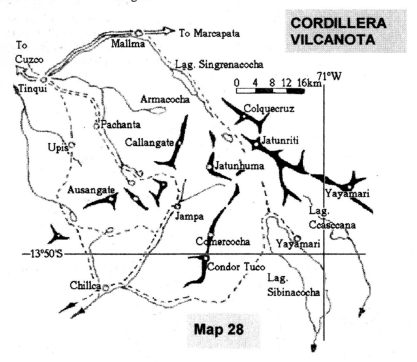

# AUSANGATE   6384m          Map 29          8 days PD+

The highest peak in SE Peru and also the highest peak of the extensive and rugged Cord.
Vilcanota. Ausangate is a great wedge shaped mountain with a dramatic N face and a gentler but
heavily glaciated slope to the S. The Indian festival of Qoyllur Riti is held every year in the
Sinakara valley to worship the gods who dwell in this important holy mountain.

**ACCESS**   From Cuzco to the village of Tinqui (3800m) (PT). Last small shops here. From
Tinqui around either the W (via Upis, Pucacocha and Ausangatecocha) or the E side (via
Pacchanta, Pachaspata and Jampa) of Ausangate to reach a base camp (4800m) in the unnamed
valley on the S side of the mountain above Pinaya, either way 3d.

**CLIMB**   The normal route is on the E flank of the mountain. From base camp go up the narrow
block filled valley on LHS of the Ausangate - Mariposa glacier. Climb scree slopes and pass the
cliff above by a series of ledges on the R at about 5000m (difficult to find but marked) to gain
easier ground and moraines. Go through the rock band at the top of the moraines in a series of
easy zigzags to reach a high camp (5450m), 5h. From the camp climb the LHS of glacier,
avoiding ice fall to reach a large glacier platform under the headwall. Climb headwall on steep
snow to gain  summit plateau  at 6000m then over easier ground to the summit. A higher camp
on the plateau edge may be needed, especially if there is heavy snow on the plateau.

**BEST MAP**   PIGM sheet 28-t 'Ocongate', 1:100,000

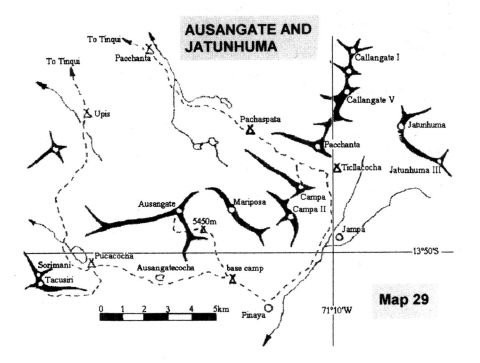

AUSANGATE AND JATUNHUMA

Map 29

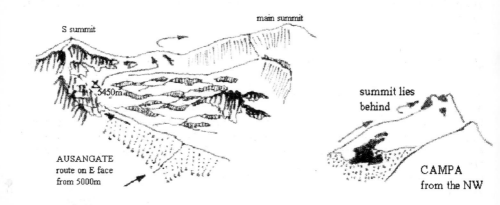

S summit

main summit

5450m

AUSANGATE
route on E face
from 5000m

summit lies
behind

CAMPA
from the NW

| No. **MARIPOSA**  5818m | Map 29 | 7 days  N/K |
| No. **CAMPA**  5500m | Map 29 | 5 days    F |

These two peaks can be climbed from a base camp at Pachaspata. Campa is one of the easiest peaks in the Cordillera Vilcanota, and a good acclimatisation ascent. Mariposa is a challenging peak, a narrow ridge mostly rock on the NE side, beautiful steep snow and ice on the SW side. The name is Spanish for butterfly. On the PIGM maps Mariposa is known as Sta. Catalina and Campa as Maria Huamantilla.

**ACCESS**  From Tinqui via Pacchanta to a camp by one of the many lagoons in the Pachaspata area N of Mariposa (4800m), 2d.

**MARIPOSA CLIMB**  By the N-NE side. No details of the exact route but it will be a mixture of rock and ice and fairly difficult.

**CAMPA CLIMB**   Follow the well worn trail up towards the Campa pass (5100m). Break R before the pass to gain the glacier and climb the easy N slopes to the summit, 5h.

**OTHER PEAKS**  Campa II can also be climbed from Pachaspata by the N side.

**BEST MAP**   As for Ausangate.

# CALLANGATE  6110m          Map 29          7 days  N/K

There are five main summits in the Callangate chain. The highest peak is marked as Collpa Ananta on the PIGM maps, but is often known as Callangate V. To add to the confusion it is also known as Chimboya in many sources!

**ACCESS**  From Tinqui to Lag. Armacocha at 4550m. 1d.

**CLIMB**  The first ascent in 1966 was by the W ridge. Grade n/k but will not be easy.

**OTHER PEAKS**  At the S end of the chain, **Pachanta 5727m**, can be climbed from Ticllacocha via the col to the N linking it with Ccapana. **Ccapana 5725m**, can also be climbed without great difficulty from Ticllacocha via the NE glacier with a short ice-wall to finish. Both ascents 1d.

The peak at the N end of the range, **Callangate I, 6000m**, was first climbed from the S in 1957, mixed snow and rock, not easy.
**BEST MAP** As Ausangate.

# JATUNHUMA 6093m          Map 29          7 days N/K

Also known as Pico Tres on the PIGM map.
**ACCESS** From Tinqui via Pacchanta and Pachaspata to Lag. Ticllacocha at 4800m, 2d.
**CLIMB** From Ticllacocha climb the wide glacier flowing down from the W side of Jatunhuma. High camp at c.5300m. Then climb by the NW buttress, the line of the first ascent in 1957. Steep snow and ice and problems getting through seracs about 150m below summit. 2-3d. from base.
**OTHER PEAKS** The subsidiary peaks to the S, Jatunhuma II and III are relatively easy ascents from the glacier plateau on their NE flanks, which is reached from Ticllacocha by going around the S side of the peaks.
**BEST MAP** As Ausangate.

JATUNHUMA from the SW

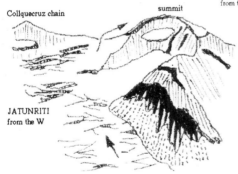

Collquecruz chain

summit

JATUNRITI from the W

# JATUNRITI 6106m          Map 28          4 days N/K

This is the peak lying about 6km ENE of Jatunhuma sometimes also known as Nañaloma or Yanaloma, but marked on the PIGM map as Chumpe. The name means big snow peak.
**ACCESS** From Mallma on the road about 20km E of Tinqui past Singrenacocha then up to a high camp by Lag. Huarurumicocha (4970m) in the broad valley W of the peak, 1d.
**CLIMB** By the large glacier N and E of Lag. Huarurumicocha to the broad col (c.5800m) N of the summit. A steep ice pitch leads to the long gentle N ridge. Grade probably about AD. 1d.

**OTHER PEAKS**  A subsidiary peak called **Colquecruz 6102m** (known as Alcamarinayoc on PIGM) lies to the NW. First ascent was by NW slopes from a base camp at 4800m. Grade likely to be about D or TD.
**BEST MAP**  As Ausangate.

# YAYAMARI  6049m               Map 28               12 days  N/K

This is the remote peak lying about 12km SE of Jatunriti and marked on the PIGM map as No. Montura. The name Yayamari means father of the little lakes.
**ACCESS**  Long and difficult but probably best as for Ausangate to the village of Chillca then on to the settlement of Yayamari at the N end of the huge Lag. Sibinacocha. Then E towards the peak. 4-5d from Tinqui valley. The direct route from the N via Singrenacocha crosses high glaciers and is not suitable for pack animals.
**CLIMB**  The first ascent was from the S and the second (in 1983!) was from the NW. The peak has big and complicated glaciers but appears to be easier angled than most Vilcanota peaks.
**BEST MAP**  PIGM sheet 28-u, 'Corani' 1:100,000, sheet 28-t 'Ocongate' useful for access.

# OTHER RANGES               Map 27

Between the Cordillera Vilcanota and the Cordillera Apolobamba are a number of isolated and remote massifs. Few mountains in these ranges will have had second ascents and many of the less prominent peaks probably await first ascents.

### CORDILLERA LA RAYA
Lying due south of the main Vilcanota range, with peaks from 5000-5500m. Access to the peaks in the SW part of range is relatively easy due to the proximity of the Cuzco - Juliaca railway which runs SW of the range. Many peaks are relatively easy and ascents can be on either snow or rock. e.g. **Yana Cuchilla 5472m** from Abra La Raya (NW of Santa Rosa) by rocky N ridge or **Cunurana 5420m** from the village of Santa Rosa by easy snow and ice on S face.

### CORDILLERA CARABAYA
This is the name generally given to the compact and rugged range lying N and E of the town of Macusani. The highest peaks are **Allincapac 5780m** (also known as Schio) and **Chichicapac 5635m**. Access from the city of Juliaca via Macusani. From the road 4km N of Macusani follow the valley NW for about 10-12km to a base camp 5km W of Chichicapac. Both peaks were first climbed from here, Chichicapac by the W ridge, Allincapac by the E face.

### CORDILLERA ARICOMA
This is the name normally used for the range lying E of Macusani and N of the river Carabaya, leading towards the Cord. Apolobamba. Access to the W is via Macusani road, access to the E end is better from Juliaca via the town of Ananea which lies S of the peaks. One of the highest peaks is **Quenamari 5294m** but sometimes given 5850m. This peak lies SE of Macusani and is an easy climb from the mine on the NE slopes. Further E, in a very remote part of Peru, is the high peak of **Aricoma 5350m**, best climbed from a pass to the N (Ananea to Limbani road).

# BOLIVIA

## INTRODUCTION

Included in this section are almost all peaks in Bolivia, including the whole of the Cordillera Apolobamba which is shared with Peru. Peaks on or near the Chilean border (including Sajama the highest in Bolivia) are part of the Cordillera Occidental and are included in that section. The ranges are described as usual from N to S, starting with the Apolobamba, followed by the Cordilleras Real, Quimsa Cruz and Lipez (see map 29).

By far the most popular range is the Cordillera Real, particularly the southern end and the peaks of Illimani, Huayna Potosi and Condoriri. This popularity is largely due to easy access but the range is also a very amenable one with several dramatic 6000m peaks which have relatively easy ascents by their normal routes. Also relatively busy are the northern Cordillera Real around Ancohuma and Illampu. Other areas of the Cordillera Real are generally very quiet due to difficult access. The Cordillera Lipez, Cordillera Apolobamba and the Quimsa Cruz are extremely quiet and only very sketchy information is available. That given here should be treated with a little respect.

## GETTING THERE

No direct flights are available to La Paz from anywhere in Europe though Lufthansa fly with a change of plane at Lima. The best options from Europe are with American Airlines via Miami, with Varig via Sao Paulo or with several carriers (Lufthansa, Iberia) via Lima. From the USA there are daily flights from Miami.

## SEASON

Climbing in all areas is best from May to August. This is winter so temperatures are very low, but it is the dry season and rain and clouds are at a minimum. Climbing is still reasonable in September and October. Most snowfall is in the summer months of December to April. The Cordillera Lipez are dry enough for climbing to be possible all year round.

## CLIMBING CONDITIONS

Most of the peaks in the Cordillera Real, Apolobamba and Quimsa Cruz are alpine in nature and ascents are normally largely on glaciers, though the Quimsa Cruz are reported to have good rock routes. In dry years the mountains can become very icy due to low winter temperatures and may be considerably harder. Snow is very stable in the Cordillera Real and avalanches are almost never seen in season. The Apolobamba have a wetter climate and fresh snow is more likely to be encountered.

## OTHER GUIDE BOOKS

Backpacking in Peru and Bolivia, 6th Ed., Bradt Publications
Formerly available in La Paz, the Spanish language guide book by Mesili 'La Cordillera Real de Los Andes', pub. Los Amigos Del Libro, La Paz
Southern Cordillera Real by Pecher and Schmiemann, pub. Plata, Switzerland, out of date and very hard to find.

# LA PAZ   The capital city of Bolivia and a good base          3700m

Most visiting mountaineers base themselves in La Paz. It makes an excellent base, particularly for the southern Cordillera Real. At an altitude of 3700m it is very good for acclimatisation though some are ill for several days on arrival. It has an international airport, all the facilities of a capital city, cheap hotels, good restaurants. Roadheads for most peaks in the Cordillera Real can be reached in a few hours, sometimes on public transport. Tourist trips to the pre-Inca ruins at Tiwanaku, the islands of the legendary Lake Titicaca and Chacaltaya mountain (5395m) can all be recommended while acclimatising

**FOOD**   There are good markets in the budget hotel area around Sagarnaga and Santa Cruz or try the Mercado Lanza near the bottom of Graneros. For supermarkets try the affluent suburbs a long way downhill.

**FUEL**   Kerosene can be bought on Calle Gallardo, directly uphill from Sagarnaga or at the neighbourhood pump on Plaza Alexander. There are several petrol stations in the middle of town. Expensive Camping Gas from the agencies mentioned below.

**MOUNTAIN TRANSPORT AND INFORMATION**   Try Guarachi, Edif. Sta Anita, Plaza Alonzo de Mendoza, or Club Andino Boliviano, Calle Mexico 1638. There are also several agencies at Sagarnaga 189 - Andean Summits recommended. Several hotels in La Paz are frequented by mountaineers and they are a good source of up to date information and climbing partners. Try the Residencial Rosario, Hotel Vienna and Hotel Italia.

**CLIMBING EQUIPMENT**   Try the notice boards of hotels mentioned above or the several agencies in the shopping centre at Sagarnaga 189 for rented or 2nd hand gear.

# CHAUPI ORCO   6044m          Map 31          8 days   PD

Chaupi Orco lies on the Peruvian-Bolivian border and is the highest point of the Cordillera Apolobamba. The range lies to the NE of Lake Titicaca, about 250km N of La Paz and some and 300km SE of Cuzco. Vicuñas are a common sight in this part of Bolivia. The Apolobamba are more heavily glaciated and prone to poorer weather than the Cordillera Real. The area from Chaupi Orco S to the area around the peaks of Soral, Azucarani and Katantica is largely an ice plateau. Chaupi Orco means 'central mountain'.

**ACCESS**   Access to Chaupi Orco is difficult but easiest via the small town of Pelechuco. (3600m). Occasional trucks or buses from La Paz. From Pelechuco it is a 3d walk to El Rincon (4300m) in the valley E of the peak, crossing three passes of 4700m E of the peak Soral. It is also possible to reach the Peruvian side of the peak from the city of Juliaca. Approach via the village of Ananea. Small stores reported in Ananea.

**CLIMB**   From Rincon establish a high camp by a small lake at the E edge of the glacier (5100m). From here go due W to pick up SSE ridge. Follow this to the summit passing or turning several minor difficulties. Ascents have also been made from the E. No details are known of the exact route or the difficulty.

**OTHER PEAKS**   Brief details of some other ascents in the area follow. **Chaupi Orco Norte 6000m, PD** has been climbed from El Rincon by the SE face, and **Soral Oeste 5641m** by the W ridge. **Soral Este 5471m** can be climbed from a camp in the valley to the N by the N ridge. To

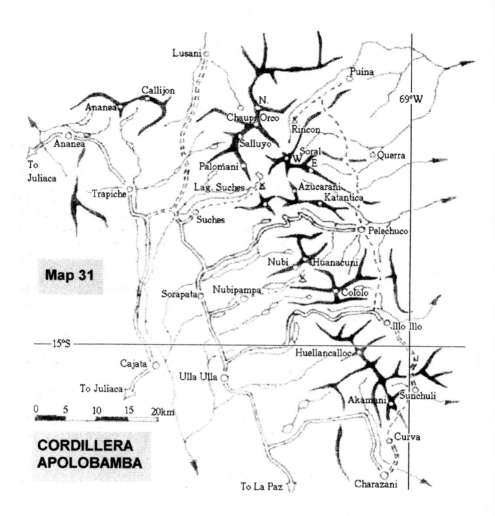

Map 31

15°S

0    5    10    15    20km

CORDILLERA
APOLOBAMBA

the SW, **Salluyo 5808m** has been climbed from the E finishing on the SE ridge. **Palomani 5768m** can be climbed by SW ridge from the village of Suches on rock and snow. **Azucarani 5580m** is a beautiful snow pyramid, first climbed by the NW ridge.

In the Peruvian Apolobamba the peaks of **Ananea 5842m** and **Callijon 5827m** can be climbed from the S.

**BEST MAP** PIGM - Sheet titled La Rinconada 1:100,000, available in Lima. No Bolivian map available. Good map of Chaupi Orco to Katantica area in AAJ 1960.

CHAUPI ORCO from the SE

## COLOLO  5915m            Map 31              8 days  N/K

Cololo is the highest peak in the southern Cordillera Apolobamba and one of the  most beautiful.
It is a more accessible and better known peak in this otherwise remote and little known range.
**ACCESS**  Access is difficult without hired transport and is expensive with! There appear to be
occasional trucks or buses going from La Paz via Ulla Ulla (4300m) to Pelechuco which can be
used for access to the range. To get to a base camp for Cololo turn  E off the road about 15km  N
of Ulla Ulla to reach the village of Nubipampa. 5km higher are camps by small lakes.
**CLIMB**  Climb by W glacier then use a hidden rock ramp to reach W ridge. Ice steps up to 70°
on the exposed ridge. Ascents have also been made from the S. Grade n/k.
**OTHER PEAKS**  To the N, **Nubi 5710m**, can be climbed from the same base area. Much
further S, one of the easiest Apolobamba peaks is **Akamani 5700m**, which can be climbed by
the SE ridge in  several days from the village of Curva.
**BEST MAP**  Sketch  map in South American Explorer issue 22.

## No. ILLAMPU  6368m          Map 33            6 days AD+

A difficult high peak in the Sorata massif at the extreme northern end of the Cordillera Real.
Illampu was first climbed in 1928.
**ACCESS**  From La Paz via Sorata (2700m)(PT) - last food and fuel. Then continue to the
village of Ancohuma (3800m). Follow valley S and SW to  gain the N glacier coming down
between Schulze and Illampu (4700m).  Continue up RHS of glacier to a high camp in the basin
under P. Schulze at 5600m. 2d.
**CLIMB**  The normal route is by the **W ridge, AD+**. There is a steep section of  45/55° snow
and ice to gain the ridge from the upper basin of the N glacier.
**OTHER ROUTES**   Many harder routes have
been climbed including **E face direct, D-** 50/60°
and  **NE face and ridge, D**.
**OTHER PEAKS**   A subsidiary summit to the N,
**Pico Del Norte 6070m**. The normal route is on the
W face at about AD. Also possible from the same
high camp is **Pico Schulze 5943m PD+**, climbed
most easily by the SE ridge but with harder routes.
**BEST MAP** Alpenvereinskarte Nr 0/8, Cordillera
Real - Nord, 1:50,000 or BIGM sheet   5846-I
'Sorata' 1:50,000

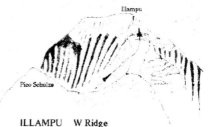

ILLAMPU   W Ridge

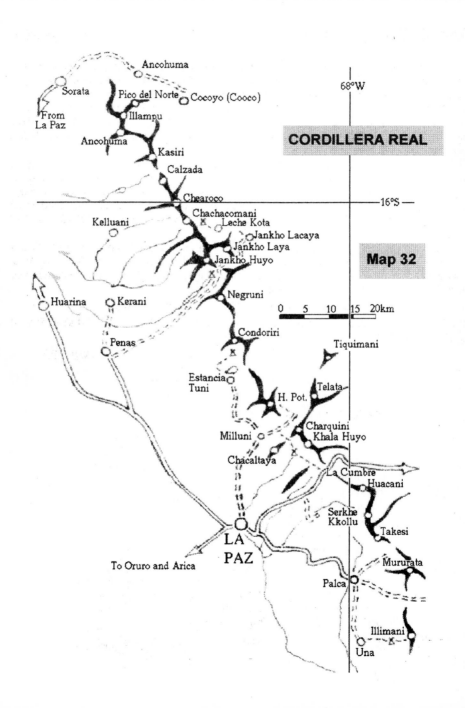

# ANCOHUMA  6427 m        Map 33            6 days PD+

Ancohuma is the highest point of the Sorata massif. Its height has been disputed but reports in the 1970's that it was 7014m high were greatly exaggerated though they did achieve credibility in the Times Atlas. The native spelling of Jankhouma, and similar variations, are often used.

**ACCESS**  The normal approach from La Paz is via Sorata (PT) where transport can be hired for trip to the road end at Mina Candelaria. Then descend to village of Cocoyo (3500m), where animals can be hired. From here walk up the valley to a base camp in the high basin (4800m) with many lakes E of the peak. 2d.

**CLIMB**  There are two normal routes, the SW ridge and the NW ridge. The **SW ridge** is gained by a steep pitch or two of ice after crossing the glacier basin (and poorly defined SE ridge) above the lakes (another high camp may be necessary). Then follow the exposed SW ridge to the summit. The **NW ridge** is also gained from the glacier above the lakes. Climb a broad snow ramp leading onto the NE ridge then make a rising traverse across the N flank. The NW ridge route is mostly snow with some III-IV rock

**OTHER ROUTES**  The SW ridge can also be reached from Lag. San Francisco to the S. This is quicker but with more objective danger. There is also a direct route on the W face from Mina Susana (4300m), about AD. Intermediate camps by a lagoon at the glacier edge (5000m) and on the high W glacier (5900m), finishing on the SW ridge.

**OTHER PEAKS**  Try **No. Jankhopiti 5875m, PD** climbed by the N ridge.

**BEST MAP**  Alpenvereinskarte # 0/8, Cordillera Real - Nord, 1:50,000 or BIGM sheet 5846-II 'Warizata' 1:50,000

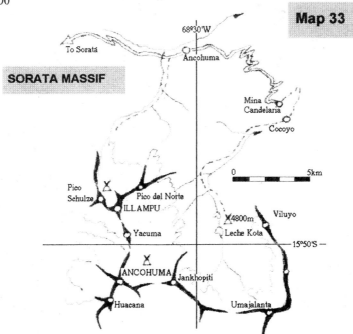

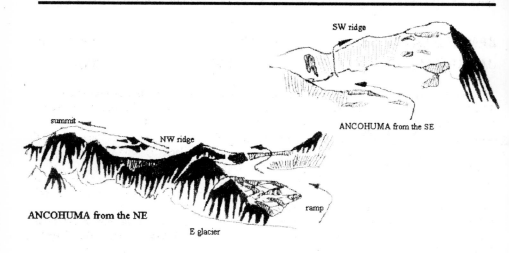

ANCOHUMA from the SE

ANCOHUMA from the NE

## No. CHEAROCO 6104 m    Map 32    6 days  AD
## No. CHACHACOMANI 5998 m    Map 32    4 days  PD

Chachacomani is the highest peak in the Andes not to make 6000m! Both peaks are rarely climbed due to the difficult access and lack of information. Due to problems with natives these peaks are now safest from the new road beyond the Khara Khota valley which passes SE of them.
**ACCESS**    From La Paz via Peñas and the Khara Khota valley, then on the new road past the peak Jankho Laya to reach the settlement of Jankho Lacaya. From here walk to Leche Kota for Chachacomani and on from here via Palca to the upper Chiquini valley for Chearoco. The peaks were climbed in the past from the W by the Kelluani river to a base camp at 5000m.
**CHEAROCO CLIMB**    The normal route is the **S-SW flank** now gained from Chekapa Kucha at the E glacier edge (5100m) by a long traverse. This is a fairly steep glacier climb about AD. The **SE flank** is reported to be a technically easier but more complex route, with a series of short 60° steps. The **E face D+** gives a harder climb, 55°.
**CHACHACOMANI CLIMB**    Normal route is now from above Leche Kota by the **E slopes, PD**. From a camp at 5500m climb moraine then a neck of snow, 45° to reach the upper glacier basin. Climb out of this by the 100m 45° headwall. There are also easy routes by the W side from the Kelluani valley. The **N face, AD** has also been climbed with ice to 50° and rock to IV.
**OTHER PEAKS**    To the N **Calzada, 5650m PD/AD,** can be climbed by the W slopes from a camp at the head of the Calzada valley.
**BEST MAP**    BIGM sheet 5946-III which covers the peaks is not currently available. Best available is the 1995 Cordillera Real map by Liam P. O'Brien, 1:135,000

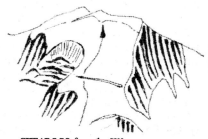

CHEAROCO from the SW

| **JANKHO LAYA** | 5545 m | Map 32 | 3 days | F |
|---|---|---|---|---|
| **JANKHO HUYO** | 5512 m | Map 32 | 2 days | F |

These peaks make excellent objectives for a short expedition or for an acclimatisation ascent.
**ACCESS**   From La Paz via Peñas to the Natividad mine (4800m) near the head of the Khara Kota valley, where a base camp can be set up by the beautiful Lag. Jankho Kota.
**JANKHO HUYO CLIMB**   From Lag. Jankho Kota follow the main valley to the pass SE of Jankho Huyo. Climb easily through rock outcrops to reach the glacier (5200m) then follow the broad SE ridge to the summit.
**JANKHO LAYA CLIMB**   Cross the pass (4980m) at the head of the Khara Kota valley by the 4WD track and continue down to a pleasant camp (4600m) at the foot of the SE ridge. Normal route is on the SE ridge, over scree then glacier.
**OTHER PEAKS** The many other peaks around these two summits provide interesting climbs at a variety of standards. Amongst the easiest are **Culin Thojo 5368m, F** and **Wila Llojeta 5244m, F.** Many of the others including **Negruni 5468m** and **Warawarani 5542m** present short technical challenges.
**BEST MAP** BIGM sheet 5945-IV, 1:50,000

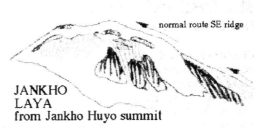

normal route SE ridge

JANKHO
LAYA
from Jankho Huyo summit

# Co. CONDORIRI    5648m            Map 32            3 days   AD

Condoriri is one of the most beautiful peaks in Bolivia, quite possibly in the entire Andes. It is climbed by a sensational route, is fairly easy to reach and is justifiably popular.
**ACCESS**   From La Paz via Estancia Tuni (4400m) where animals can be hired. Getting here is difficult without a vehicle.  From Tuni go around S end of the large Lag. Tuni, then turn N and follow valley to Lag. Chiar Kota (4700m)
**CLIMB**   The normal route **SW ridge, AD** from Lag. Chiar Kota. Follow path N to a hidden wide scree couloir through the rock band. Follow this couloir up L to reach the Condoriri glacier (SW of summit). Climb this glacier towards summit pyramid. Climb up to the ridge by a 40/50° gully through a rock band to reach a prominent notch. Then follow the very airy ridge to summit.
**OTHER ROUTES** The **S face D+** climbed direct, 55°.  The subsidiary peak to the north, the **Ala Norte 5540m** has been climbed by the **SE face D-**, 50/55°
**OTHER PEAKS** The subsidiary peak to the E **Pequeño Alpamayo c.5400m, PD** is a beautiful snow pyramid. Ascend from SW (Lag. Chiar Kota) by SW glacier then SW ridge.
**BEST MAP** BIGM 1:50,000, sheets 5945-II and 5945-III

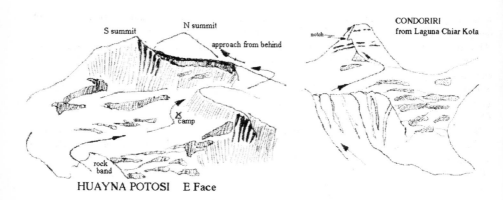

HUAYNA POTOSI   E Face

# Co. HUAYNA POTOSI   6094m     Map 32     3 days   PD

A fine isolated triangular peak which dominates the view as you come in to land at La Paz airport. There are two summits, the N is slightly higher, the S a slightly more difficult climb. Reputedly the easiest 6000'er in the Cordillera Real but in some years Illimani may be easier. The impressive and accessible W face has a large number of long and difficult routes. Also known as Cacca Aca.

**ACCESS**   Hire private transport all the way to Zongo Pass (no PT). There is now a refugio here, all facilities but not much space.

**CLIMB**   From Lag. Zongo, cross the dam and follow an aqueduct to a small stream. Ascend this through moraines, then go L to a prominent moraine rib. Trend L up broken rock behind to gain the glacier at 5200m and cross this in a wide RH arc to the snow ridge on R coming down from the S summit. Underneath this is Camp Argentino at c.5500m (6h. from dam). Higher camps are possible. From the camp climb up steep slope above and then easier snow slopes to pass under E slope of the summit. Gain the N ridge and follow this back to the summit, exposed but easy.

**OTHER ROUTES**   The S peak is harder, about PD+ and can also be climbed from Camp Argentino. There are also several routes on the imposing 1000m W face, all about D and 55-60°.

**OTHER PEAKS**   To the N is **Tiquimani 5519m**, (called Illampu on BIGM maps). This is a very hard mountain. Normal route is on the mixed SW face, at least TD, 60/65° and V/VI. Peak to W called **Maria Lloco, 5522m**. Approach via Milluni to ridge above and S of Carmen Pampa. Follow aqueduct to glacier. Go up glacier and curve round behind rocky spur to climb by NE ridge. **Charquini 5392m, F.** Normally climbed from Lag. Zongo by NW glacier after a spectacular walk along the aqueduct. Other routes look possible from the SW glacier.

**BEST MAP**   BIGM 1:50,000, sheet 5945-II

# CHACALTAYA  5395m          Map 32               1 day     F
# WILA MANKILISANI  5324m     Map 32               2 days   PD

Two lower peaks which make ideal acclimatisation ascents. Many companies offer day tours to Chacaltaya from La Paz, driving up to 5180m where there is a ski-tow. The mountain also makes a fine easy day out from the far side. The two peaks can be climbed as a combination from a high camp in the Kaluyo valley. Wila Mankilisani is sometimes known as Khala Huyo.

**ACCESS**   To get to the Kaluyo valley from La Paz take a bus or a taxi up the tar road to La Cumbre pass (4800m)(PT) 1h. Walk W over low pass and descend into Kaluyo valley. Good camping at lagoons. 2h.

**WILA MANKILISANI CLIMB**   Climb LHS of rectangular SW glacier (30-40°) then an easy 10m gully right in the corner of the glacier to reach ridge. Climb shattered rock ridge (II) turning first pinnacle on RHS. Easier to summit. 4h.

**CHACALTAYA CLIMB**   Take day tour from La Paz to Club Andino lodge at 5180m and stroll easily to the summit. Can also be climbed from Kaluyo valley camps in about 6h.. No snow. Ridge to N of peak makes a fine walking traverse.

**OTHER PEAKS** Several other peaks are   worthwhile.   **Telata   5336m.** Climb direct by the glacier on the SW flank to a notch, then L over snow and scree to the summit. About PD.

**BEST MAP**   BIGM 1:50,000 sheet 5945-II for Wila Mankilisani, sheet 5944-I for Chacaltaya

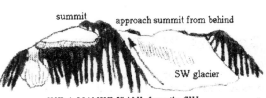

WILA MANKILISANI from the SW

# SERKHE KKOLLU 5546m        Map 32              2 days N/K

**ACCESS**   About 15km out of town on the way to La Cumbre is Lag. Incachaca. Take the track from here over ridge to the E and a second larger lake, Lag. Challapata (4200m).

**CLIMB**   Follow valley up and E from Challapata to Lag. Serkhe Kota (4800m), ½d. Climb from here, 1d., grade and exact route n/k.

**OTHER PEAKS**   Further N is **Huacani 5321m**. Follow valley up from Challapata, turning slowly E and passing two lakes to camp, ½d. From here climb the main peak which lies to the N, 1d. Some snow, crampons possibly needed, difficulty n/k, but probably not hard.

**BEST MAP**   BIGM 1:50,000, sheet 6044-IV

# MURURATA 5869m              Map 32              3 days   F

In legend the god Thunupa was angered by the arrogant Mururata. He knocked off the head of Mururata with his catapult and it became Sajama. Mururata was left headless and the flat topped summit is prominent from La Paz to this day! One of the easiest peaks in the Cord. Real.

**ACCESS**   From La Paz use 4WD to drive to Estancia Choquekota via Huancapampa. Turn E off this road and go up the large valley to E on old trails to base camp at snow line (4900m), 1d.

**CLIMB**   Climb to the summit by the easy angled glacier which can be arduous in deep snow. Mururata is a good ski-mountaineering ascent.

**BEST MAP**   Alpenverienskarte # 0/9 1:50,000. Or, BIGM 1:50,000 sheet 6044-III

# No. ILLIMANI Pico Sur  6462m          Map 32          4 days PD+

The highest peak of the Cordillera Real and a mountain which dominates La Paz. Illimani is a fine long ridge running NW-SE, continuously over 6000m for 8km, with the highest point near the S end. Large glaciers descend its flanks to c.4600m. First ascended by Conway in 1898. The first traverse over the full ridge was done in 1972.

**ACCESS**   Normally from La Paz via Palca to Estancia Una (3600m). Pack animals can be hired here for the 4h. walk to base camp (4400m) at Puente Roto. Puente Roto can also be reached from the N  by an old 4WD mine road (blocked 8km to the N) and then level walking for 8km.

**CLIMB**    From Puente Roto climb screes to pass a rock band (4800m) on R. Up to col in the ridge to S (4900m).  Continue up the rock ridge which becomes steeper and more exposed (I-II) to reach Nido de Condores camp (5450m), 4-6h. From here go up the small forepeak and follow the ridge to levelling and  possible high camp (5800m) then up the shoulder above avoiding crevasses and ice walls. Usually fairly easy, but sometimes with one or two serious ice pitches. Move L at top to gain the summit ridge N of  the summit. Follow the fine summit ridge S.

**OTHER ROUTES**  Routes on the **N peak** include one directly below the summit on steep snow by **SW face, D- 50°**.  Gain the face by traversing from the normal S peak route at 5800m. Also by the prominent triangular snowfield to the N of the Nido D-. Illimani has also climbed by the long N ridge with both LH and RH starts D- 40/50°

**OTHER PEAKS**   SW of base camp **C. Sonaka 4615m F,** is a  half day excursion with a good view of the normal route on Illimani.

**BEST MAP**   Alpenverienskarte # 0/9 1:50,000. Or
BIGM 1:50,000  sheet 6044-III.

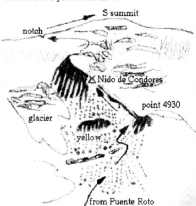

ILLIMANI S peak from the W

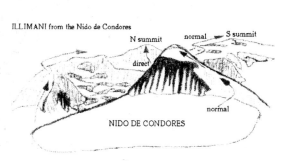

ILLIMANI from the Nido de Condores

Photo: **On the North ridge of Huayna Potosi, Cordillera Real, Bolivia.** J. Biggar.

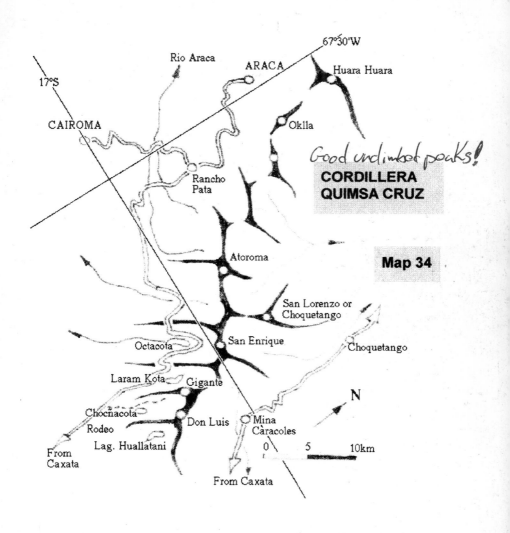

Photo: **Moonrise over Licancabur, Cordillera Occidental, Chile.** G. Biggar

## Co. GIGANTE 5748m                Map 34                6 days  F/PD

This is the highest peaks in the Quimsa Cruz range, an isolated and compact group which lie to the S of Illimani. Access to the range is not easy and very little information is available. There is generally less snow and ice than in the Cordillera Real but all the highest summits are glaciated.

**ACCESS** From La Paz to Panduro on the Oruro road then to the village of Caxata (4400m) (PT). From here access to the mountains in general can be made up mine roads, either walking driving or hitching on mine lorries. For Gigante follow a good track past Rodeo which leads to a mine at Chocñacota on the W slope of the mountains.

**CLIMB** A relatively easy ascent. Most ascents have been from the W. The normal route appears to be the S ridge gained from Lag. Laramcota by the steep W face or from the mine below Chocñacota by the gentle SE glacier. The W ridge has also been climbed.

**OTHER PEAKS** Reputedly there are many interesting lower peaks in the northern Quimsa Cruz, with some of the best quality rock in the Andes. **Atoroma 5580m** unnamed on the BIGM map, has been climbed by a snow ridge from the SW, see Neates 'Mountaineering in the Andes' for further details. The other main summits of the Quimsa Cruz are not reported to be difficult and most are easiest to get to, and climb, from the W. These include **Don Luis (Jachacunocollo) 5721m,** climbed from Chocñacota, **San Enrique 5600m,** climbed by S face on straightforward 40-50° snow and **San Lorenzo 5508m.** E of the Mina Caracoles road is another massif whose highest point is **San Roque 5520m**

**BEST MAP** BIGM sheets 6143-III (Gigante, Atoroma and Don Luis), 6142-IV and 6142-I 1:50,000, cover the highest peaks of the Cord. Quimsa Cruz

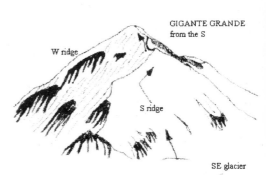

GIGANTE GRANDE from the S

W ridge

S ridge

SE glacier

## Co. UTURUNCO 6009m          Map 30          5 days     F
## Co. NUEVO MUNDO 5929m        Map 30          5 days     F

Uturunco is one of the most isolated yet easiest 6000m peaks in South America. Nuevo Mundo is the second highest summit in the remote Cordillera Lipez in SW Bolivia. Uturunco means jaguar.

**ACCESS** Access for Uturunco from Uyuni via Mallku to Quetena Chico which lies NW of the mountain. For Nuevo Mundo drive via San Pablo de Lipez to San Antonio de Lipez. Private 4WD vehicle will be essential to reach these peaks.

**UTURUNCO CLIMB** From Quetena Chico a usable vehicle track runs to about 5600m on the N flank of the mountain (mine workings). From here stroll easily up screes in 3h to the summit.

**OTHER PEAKS** Nuevo Mundo, is an easy ascent with little or no snow. There are many other easy but remote peaks in this area, some still waiting first ascents.

**BEST MAP** BIGM sheet SF-19-8, 1:250,000

# CORDILLERA OCCIDENTAL

**INTRODUCTION** *Water Problem Area: Think Well!*

The Cordillera Occidental is the name given to the chain of volcanic mountains which stretches from Arequipa in southern Peru, down the Chile-Bolivia border to the northern edge of the Puna de Atacama. The mountains are almost without exception easy volcanic ascents though a few, such as the highest peak No. Sajama, are more eroded. The mountains rise in isolation from a generally high plateau at about 4200-4400m giving splendid views from the summits. There are active volcanoes throughout the length of the range. Access can be a problem and water is almost always a problem.

The scenery in the area is superb with an enduring sense of remoteness and desolation. The air is beautifully sharp. Small villages lie scattered over the vast Altiplano, dwarfed by the volcanic peaks and battered by dust storms. In the wetter areas there are large flat swamps known as 'bofedales' where llamas and alpacas graze in their hundreds. Wildlife is easily seen and more numerous than in the classic ranges such as Cord. Blanca and Cord. Real. Vizcachas, rheas, flamingos and vicuñas are all commonly seen, the condor is occasionally seen.

## GETTING THERE

For the Peruvian Occidental the best base is Arequipa with daily flights from Lima on all three Peruvian airlines (AeroPeru, Americana and Faucett). See under northern Peru for details of flights from Europe and the USA to Lima.

For the northern Chilean Occidental either fly via Santiago to Arica or fly to La Paz and approach overland from Bolivia (see Bolivia section). There's not much to choose between these two options though the approach via La Paz has the advantage as far as acclimatisation is concerned. For the southern Chilean Occidental the best approach is to fly to Calama via Santiago. See under the High Andes for details of flights to Santiago.

## SEASON

Ascents can be made of all the peaks in the Cordillera Occidental at any time of year. The area has a very dry climate and although it experiences the same summer wet season as the rest of Peru and Bolivia (December - April) the quantities of snow are so small that climbing is not badly affected. Recent storms may reduce water problems due to the presence of a lower snow line.

## CLIMBING CONDITIONS

This is a very dry area. Water is hard to obtain on many peaks until the snow line is reached. Only the highest peaks, over 6000m, have permanent snowfields or glaciers. Penitentes can be bad reaching as high as 5m on some peaks and making travel 'against the grain' almost impossible. Navigating across almost flat summit plateaux can also be a problem.

Snow is generally very stable provided there has been no recent fall from a storm. It does not normally turn soft later in the day. Hard windslab can be found high on some of the peaks. Approaches over ash and scree can be arduous.

## OTHER GUIDE BOOKS        None known

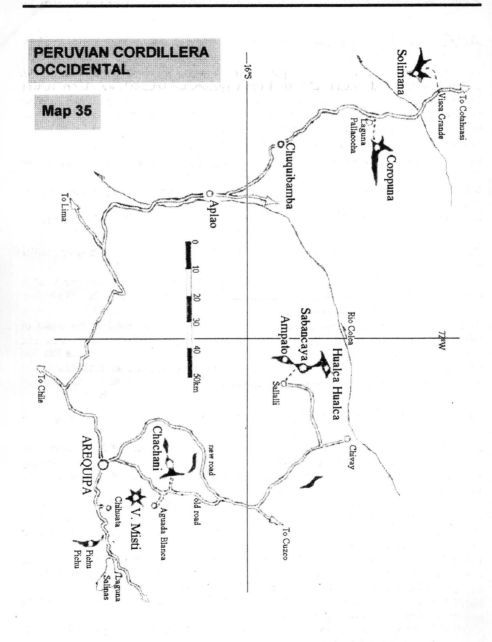

PERUVIAN CORDILLERA OCCIDENTAL

Map 35

# AREQUIPA   The main city of SW Peru          2325m

Arequipa is a pleasant and relatively prosperous city in southern Peru. It sits in an oasis at 2325m at the foot of the volcano El Misti. There is a particularly beautiful Plaza de Armas, with El Misti forming a stunning backdrop. The nearby Colca canyon is worth a visit. There are many organised tours to this vast canyon which is supposedly the deepest canyon in the world. It is one of the best places in the Andes to see condors.

**FOOD** There is a good supermarket on the SW corner of the Plaza de Armas.

**FUEL** Kerosene can be bought at S end of La Merced. There are many petrol stations around the central area. Camping gas has never been seen.

**MOUNTAIN INFORMATION** A good source is Carlos Zarate who can be contacted at the Alliance Francaise opposite Santa Catalina or PO Box 2480

**MOUNTAIN TRANSPORT** Try tour agencies towards N end of Jerusalen or Carlos Zarate.

# No. SOLIMANA 6093m          Map 35          5 days  N/K

A steep and eroded volcanic massif with an impressive S face overlooking the deep Chichas canyon. There are four main peaks on a ridge running for 1km roughly NE to SW. The highest point is at or near the SW end of this ridge.

**ACCESS** From Arequipa as for Coropuna but continue towards the village of Cotahuasi for 30km to the next pass at Visca Grande (4650m)(PT). From here walk W, then SW to reach huts at Sora on the N slope of the mountain.

**CLIMB** Up N or NW side, including glacier from 5300m, steep snow and ice, grade n/k.

**BEST MAP** PIGM Sheet 31-q 'Cotahuasi', 1:100,000.

# No. COROPUNA 6425m          Map 35          5 days          F

A complex volcanic mountain plateau with an 8km plateau-ridge over 6000m in height. The peak on SW corner of the plateau, known as Bingham, appears to be the highest but this may vary with snow build up. The name means 'shrine on the plateau'. Remains of clothing from Inca ascents have been found as high as 6000m.

**ACCESS** Easiest from Arequipa in southern Peru via the small town of Chuquibamba (3000m - last food and fuel) then along the Cotahuasi road (PT) to Lag. Pallacocha (4750m). This lagoon can't be seen from road but is at highest point of road when the road is nearest to Coropuna. 8h drive from Arequipa.

**CLIMB** The highest point is just behind the RH of two domes seen from Pallacocha. Normal route on this peak is by W rib. High camps can be made at 5600-5800m, 1d. then follow RH of two prominent rock ribs and glacier slopes above (small crevasses only). Go over foresummit and on to highest point. Navigation would be very difficult in cloud. Coropuna can probably be climbed from several other directions just as easily.

**OTHER PEAKS** Other peaks of the Coropuna massif would make interesting ascents and a ski traverse would be a real expedition.

**BEST MAP** PIGM sheet 32-q, 'Chuquibamba', 1:100,000

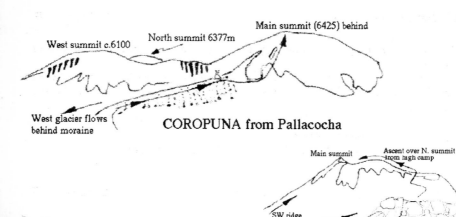

West summit c.6100
North summit 6377m
Main summit (6425) behind
West glacier flows behind moraine

COROPUNA from Pallacocha

Main summit
Ascent over N. summit from high camp
SW ridge
Lava in foreground
Approach to high camp

AMPATO from Sallalli

| | | | | |
|---|---|---|---|---|
| **No. AMPATO** 6288m | Map 35 | 5 days | F |
| **No. HUALCA HUALCA** 6025m | Map 35 | 4 days | N/K |
| **No. SABANCAYA** 5976m | Map 35 | 4 days | F |

Three volcanoes in a remote setting only 100km from Arequipa. Sabancaya was erupting, throughout the early 1990's, throwing off a plume of ash every 2h in 1994. Hualca Hualca is extinct. A ceremonial puma skin was found high on Hualca Hualca in the 1980's. The name Ampato means frog. In 1995 the rapidly retreating glacier on Ampato revealed the corpse of a young girl killed by a sharp blow to the skull approximately 500 years ago.

**ACCESS**   Easiest from Arequipa along Chivay road (PT) and then turn W to get to remote settlement of Sallalli (4400m). 6h drive. No facilities. From here gain and walk up the unnamed valley which comes down from the col between Ampato and Sabancaya. High camps can be established at about 5200m. Water flows only in the afternoons - very muddy.

**AMPATO CLIMB**   Several possible routes on the S and W sides of the mountain. Glacier now only above 6000m. This is in very poor state with many penitentes, due to ash eruptions of Sabancaya. The normal route was from the NE, over N summit but this is hard work if penitentes are bad. SW ridge is also possible - grade easy but n/k.

**HUALCA HUALCA CLIMB**   Hualca Hualca can also be reached from the Sallalli area. It is a more complex mountain with several valley glaciers. The normal route is apparently up the E glacier then N to summit - grade n/k.

**SABANCAYA CLIMB**   Sabancaya can be climbed easily using the same approach as Ampato and then up the S slopes. Ash and some ice.

**BEST MAP** PIGM, sheet 32-s, 'Chivay', 1:100,000

# No. CHACHANI 6084m          Map 35          3 days     F

A complex massif with many summits but very little snow. There are archaeological remains near the summit.
**ACCESS** From Arequipa follow the old road to Chivay, beyond Aguada Blanca. The road turns N along the E flank of the mountain to Cutipampa where a 4WD track leads W and higher (up to 4800m). No public transport.
**CLIMB** From a camp on the E flank go up rocky slopes and over point 5852m to reach the summit in one long day. No permanent snow.
**BEST MAP** PIGM sheet 33-s, 'Arequipa'. 1:100,000, Sheet 33-t for approach

# V. MISTI 5842m          Map 35          3 days     F

This perfect volcanic cone sits right above Arequipa in southern Peru. It is climbed very often and is something of a tourist mountain, people reaching the summit even in trainers and sandals. There is no water on the mountain except at the Aguada Blanca reservoir. There is usually no snow either. The mountain is another that was climbed by the Incas.
**ACCESS** Two approaches are commonly used The longer climb but easier access is from the shanty town of Apurimac San Luis (PT) on N side of Arequipa. The other approach is a 3h drive from Arequipa to Aguada Blanca which gives a height advantage. There is no water on the mountain and usually no snow either. If there is snow it will be very high.
**CLIMB** There are two normal routes. **1.** S side from Apurimac San Luis. Head for Tres Cruces (3000m) then up under pylons to Los Pastores at 3300m. From here follow the path up rib past possible camp at 4200m. 1d. Then on to summit.
**2.** An easier climb is from the reservoir of Aguada Blanca (3700m) on NE side. Head for prominent NE rib. Protected tent sites at 4600m. 1d. From here follow path which takes rising traverse up N slopes to summit. Bad scree in places. The high camp on this route can also be approached from the village of Chihuata (PT) to the S. 1d.
**BEST MAP** PIGM sheet 33-t, 'Characato', 1:100,000

# No. PICHU PICHU 5630m          Map 35          3 days     F

A long ridge which dominates Arequipa's E skyline. Remains of a young woman were found with various wooden and copper items on the summit ridge. The highest peak is the centrally located Co. Crespon Grande.
**ACCESS** From Arequipa to Lag. Salinas (flamingos) to the N of summit.
**CLIMB** Walk S then climb E slopes of the mountain, no permanent snow and very easy.
**BEST MAP** PIGM sheet 33-T, 'Characato', 1:100,000

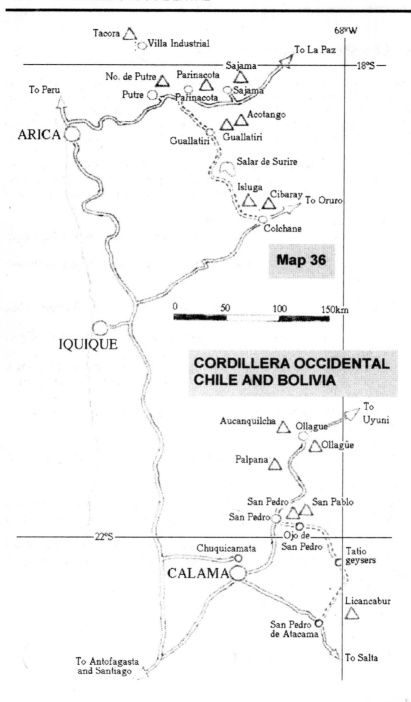

68°W

Tacora

Villa Industrial

To La Paz

Sajama

18°S

No. de Putre    Parinacota

To Peru

Putre    Parinacota

Sajama

ARICA

Acotango

Guallatiri    Guallatiri

Salar de Surire

Isluga

Cibaray    To Oruro

Colchane

**Map 36**

0    50    100    150km

IQUIQUE

**CORDILLERA OCCIDENTAL
CHILE AND BOLIVIA**

To
Uyuni

Aucanquilcha    Ollague

Ollagüe

Palpana

San Pedro    San Pablo

San Pedro

22°S

Chuquicamata    Ojo de
San Pedro

Tatio
geysers

CALAMA

Licancabur

San Pedro
de Atacama

To Antofagasta
and Santiago

To Salta

# ARICA   A Pacific port in northern Chile                    0m

Arica is the only big city in this part of Chile but being at sea level it makes a poor base for mountaineers. It is useful more as a starting point for trips into the northern Chilean Occidental and for somewhere to go swimming afterwards! Though a nice enough town, Arica does not have much to offer, but the Lauca National Park in the area around the Bolivian border containing the beautiful V. Parinacota is well worth a visit for the quality of scenery and the rare wildlife (vicuña, rhea and flamingo) which can be seen.

**GETTING THERE**   Daily flights from Santiago and La Paz. Many buses every day from Santiago (comfortable but long 28 h. journey) and about two per week from La Paz, 18 h. By 1996 the new road to La Paz should be finished all the way and this will dramatically affect transport in the area.

**FOOD**   Several large supermarkets in the centre of town.

**FUEL**   Several petrol stations, particularly COPEC, sell kerosene. No knowledge of camping gas being available.

**MOUNTAIN TRANSPORT**   For private transport to Putre, Parinacota etc., try one of the tour operators or hire a 4WD from Hertz, Budget etc.

# V. TACORA   5988m                Map 36                5 days  N/K

A famous volcano just on the Chilean side of the Peru-Chile border, visible from the city of Tacna in southern Peru but best approached from Arica in Chile

**ACCESS**   From Arica or La Paz take the train (2-3 per week) to Villa Industrial (4100m), about 40km before the border village of Visviri. From here roads (20km - condition n/k) lead to mines on the N side of the volcano at up to 5000m.

**CLIMB**   Grade not known but likely to be a very easy volcano ascent with little or no snow.

**BEST MAP**   ChIGM Sheet SE 19-6, 'Visviri', 1:250,000

# No. de PUTRE   5815m              Map 36                2 days   F

A small eroded peak NE of Putre.

**ACCESS**   From Arica to the small town of Putre at 3500m by good tar road. (PT). Putre is a pleasant town at the base of the mountain which has shops, cafes etc. and makes a good intermediate base before going higher to do peaks such as Parinacota and Guallatiri.

**CLIMB**   Possible from several directions including directly up from Putre, but probably easiest from the Lauca National Park entrance station at Las Cuevas (4500m). From here gain long NE ridge. Scree and rock.

**BEST MAP**   ChIGM sheet SE 19-10, 'Arica', 1:250,000

# V. PARINACOTA 6342m     Map 37     5 days     F
# V. POMERAPE 6222m     Map 37     5 days     F

These two peaks known collectively as the Payachatas, sit right on the Chile-Bolivia border. Under snow, Parinacota is one of the most beautiful volcanic cones and has a deep crater. Last eruption n/k but lava flows, cinder cones etc., can be seen on the volcano's southern flanks. Parinacota is Quechua for 'lake of the flamingos'. Pomerape, or Pomarata, means 'peak of the puma'

**ACCESS** Easiest from Arica in Chile though the new tar road will make access from La Paz much easier. From Arica go via Putre (3500m) to get to either Parinacota village (4500m)(PT) or Caquena. There is a mountain refuge at Parinacota with limited facilities and a small shop and cafe nearby at Chucullo. In either case walk over pumice and lava to base of one peak or to the col between the two peaks (5350m) if you wish to climb them both. 1d. Water only from snow, often as high as 5500m. The peaks can also be approached from Sajama village in Bolivia, 1d.

**PARINACOTA CLIMB** This perfect volcanic cone can be climbed easily from any direction. Snowfields on S and W sides are easier than often bare scree on N and E. Lava ribs may also offer an easier ascent than scree.

**POMERAPE CLIMB** Pomerape can be climbed from several directions. From the Chilean side the normal route is by SW flank, glaciated, about PD and possibly icy. From the Bolivian side the

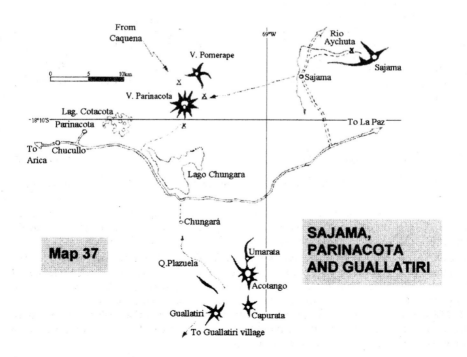

easiest route is W ridge, F. Pass the rock band at 5800m on the extreme L. Easy snow slopes with a few crevasses lead to the summit.

**OTHER PEAKS** Try **No. Condoriri 5762m, F** to the N, mostly scree but with some ice on summit. Most lower peaks have no snow and little interest.

**BEST MAP** BIGM sheet 5739-I, or ChIGM sheet SE 19-10, 'Arica', 1:250,000

# No. SAJAMA 6542m          Map 37          5 days  PD

Bolivia's highest mountain, being about 100m higher than anything in the Cord. Real. It is also the highest peak in the Cord. Occidental. Sajama is an eroded volcano with some big and unstable cliffs. It is a slightly harder ascent than any of the other major peaks in the Cord. Occidental, particularly in icy years. The village of Sajama at its base is a friendly little place with very basic shops and some lodging available.

**ACCESS** Easiest from La Paz but also possible from Arica in Chile. Get to village of Sajama (4250m)(PT). Donkeys can be hired here to the normal base camp (4800m) by the Rio Aychuta (often dry but some water can usually be found higher up). Red barked Queñoa trees near here. are said to be the highest in the world. 4h.

**CLIMB** Several possible on S, W and N sides of mountain. The normal is W, by a curving glacier above base camp to join SW ridge at c.6000m (high camp at c.5800m is possible above the bend in glacier). Also frequently climbed by the SW ridge direct for which a base on SW side of mountain may be better. In some (icy) years the NW ridge may be easier since it gets more sun. This ridge can be reached from the normal base at Aychuta. All routes about 8-10h.

**BEST MAP** BIGM, sheet 5839-IV, 1:50,000

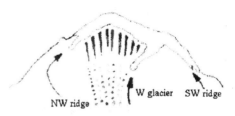

SAJAMA from the W

# V. GUALLATIRI 6063m          Map 37          5 days     F
# V. ACOTANGO 6050m          Map 37          5 days  N/K

Two volcanoes which are the highest of a group of four summits. Guallatiri is very active and erupted in 1960. It is a contender for the world's highest active volcano as it appears to be the highest volcano which has been seen to erupt lava. Guallata is Aymará for goose.

**ACCESS** Several possibilities but easiest from Chile. The mountains can be approached direct from the Arica-La Paz road (PT) at Lago Chungará about 15km to the N on the Chilean side of the border. The Q. Plazuela is normally dry. The shortest approach to V. Guallatiri is from the village of Guallatiri (4200m) to the SW - few facilities and no public transport.

**CLIMBS** Both peaks are easy volcanoes with small permanent snowfields which can be climbed from most directions. Guallatiri is recommended from the village of Guallatiri with a high camp by the snowline and is reported to have bad penitentes.

**OTHER PEAKS** The third big peak of the group is **Capurata 5990m**. The next major summits south are four or five eroded volcanoes surrounding the Salar de Surire. Not very inspiring mountains but the Salar is a beautiful place with a hot spring, drinkable water and flamingos.
**BEST MAP** ChIGM sheet SE 19-10, 'Arica', 1: 250,000

| | | | |
|---|---|---|---|
| **V. ISLUGA** 5530m | Map 36 | 5 days | F |
| **Co. CIBARAY** 5869m | Map 36 | 5 days | N/K |

Between the giant volcanoes around the Lauca National Park and the big peaks by Calama there are many lower peaks, two of the more prominent and more easily accessible are the active volcano Isluga (last eruption 1960) and Cibaray, on either side of the border by the village of Colchane (3600m). Cibaray, which is also known as Carabaya, has a 10km long summit ridge, with highest point at W end.
**ACCESS** Get transport to Colchane. Buses from Iquique to Oruro pass through Colchane (small shops and cafes) several times per week. For Isluga head to the village of Enquelga (hot springs) on the S flank of the volcano.
**CLIMBS** Isluga is best climbed from the S. Cibaray can be climbed directly from Colchane, but it's probably better to cross the border officially and climb from Pisiga in Bolivia.
**BEST MAP** ChIGM sheet SF-19-15, 'Pisiga Chile', 1:250,000.

# CALAMA  Chilean mining town in the Atacama desert        2350m

Calama is a pleasant but unexciting town in a small oasis in the middle of the Atacama desert at an altitude of 2350m. It is a useful base for climbing peaks in the southern Chilean Occidental and northern Puna de Atacama. From the airport and the outskirts there are views to Licancabur and the twin peaks of San Pedro and San Pablo. The copper mine in the nearby town of Chuquicamata makes an unusual half day sightseeing tour - this is reputedly the world's biggest hole in the ground.
**GETTING THERE** There are daily flights from Santiago. Many bus departures daily to Santiago (24h.) and also northwards to Arica etc.
**FOOD** Two supermarkets on Vargas near centre of town.
**FUEL** Petrol station on the LHS on the road out to Chuquicamata appears to be the nearest to the centre that sells kerosene.
**MOUNTAIN TRANSPORT AND INFORMATION** Try Atacama Desert Expediciones, Balmaceda 1962 or Andino Expeditions Vivar 1963.

# Co. AUCANQUILCHA  6176m     Map 38     5 days    F
# V. OLLAGÜE  5868m      Map 38     4 days    F

These two big volcanoes north of Calama both have old mine workings on them - those on Ollagüe at 5600m, those on Aucanquilcha are at 6000m. Vehicle tracks leading to these mines are now impassable higher up, but leave the peaks as very easy ascents which can even be done on a mountain bike!  No  running water on the mountains but Aucanquilcha usually has snow near the summit.

**ACCESS**   For both peaks get transport from Calama to the small village of Ollagüe (3700m) which has a couple of very primitive shops and one cafe.  No buses use this road but there is a once weekly train from Calama.

**AUCANQUILCHA CLIMB**   Aucanquilcha can be climbed from the village of Ollagüe in 4-5 days by the old mine roads on the E and NE flanks.  There was water at old settlement of Amincha in 1994.  With 4WD transport to drive to the base of the mountain  (4800m) the ascent could be done in one day. Usually some snow near the summit.

**OLLAGÜE  CLIMB**     Ollague can be climbed from the village in 3 days by the old mine road which reaches 5600m on the WNW side.  There are craters near the summit  with  fumaroles.  With  4WD transport the ascent could be done in one day from the old mining settlement at c.4500m.

**BEST MAPS** ChIGM sheets 2100-6810 and 2115-6800, 1:50,000 or sheet SF-19-7, 'Ollagüe', 1:250,000

**Map 38**

**AUCANQUILCHA, SAN PEDRO AND SAN PABLO**

# Co. PALPANA  6022m        Map 38              4 days     F

A big and easy volcano about half way between Aucanquilcha and San Pedro, lying E of the beautiful Salar de Ascotan, on which there are many flamingos.

**ACCESS**   As for Aucanquilcha but stop about 35km before Ollagüe at the NW corner of the Salar de Ascotan (3700m). Watch out for the minefield here.

**CLIMB**   From here Palpana can be climbed easily either by the E scree slopes direct or  via the broad col which lies N of the mountain.
**BEST MAP**   ChIGM sheet  SF-19-7, 'Ollagüe', 1:250,000 or 1:50,000 sheet (number n/k)

# V. SAN PEDRO   6154m        Map 38                6 days      F
# V. SAN PABLO   6118m        Map 38                6 days      F

A pair of very high volcanoes N of Calama and seen from the outskirts of the city. San  Pedro is active and like many volcanoes in the Cord. Occidental last erupted in 1960. No water on the mountains and snow only very near summits.
**ACCESS**   From Calama there are several possibilities. The easiest is probably via Estacion San Pedro (PT) then take minor road 20km E to the Ojo de San Pedro (3750m) on the S side of the mountains. There is water here - a good base camp.  Volcanoes could also be approached from N but no water.
**CLIMB**   Both peaks can be  easily climbed from  the Ojo de San Pedro via the  high col between them (5200m).
**OTHER PEAKS**   Immediately south of these two volcanoes are several high peaks including **Paniri 5960m, F** which can be  climbed by NW slopes  from Ojo de San Pedro. There are extensive ruins on the summit.
**BEST MAP**   ChIGM  1:50,000, sheet(s) not known or sheet  SF-19-7, 'Ollagüe', 1:250,000.

# V. LICANCABUR   5916m             Map 40                    4 days      F

Licancabur is a perfect isolated cone  with archaeological remains on the summit and a crater lake which is usually frozen. The world's highest sub-aqua dive was done here in search of Inca treasure. It is climbed relatively often for an Atacama volcano. There is no drinking water on any of the peaks in this area and often no snow either. To the NE of Licancabur, in Bolivia, the Lag. Verde is very beautiful but full of undrinkable brine.
There are regular tours from San Pedro and Calama to the geysers at Tatio (4400m), which are worth a visit. With free hot baths and drinkable water they would make a good base for acclimatisation or climbing  a few smaller peaks in the immediate area.
**ACCESS**   A map appears in the next chapter. From Calama there are two commonly used approaches. Both are via the village of San Pedro de Atacama first, a nice place but with many tourists (PT). Vehicles can be hired here very easily. **1.** A very rough track runs up the W side of the mountain to the col (4400m) between Licancabur and Sairecabur. It is passable in 4WD to about 3900m.  Watch out for minefields at the col. **2.** The S side of Licancabur and Juriques can be reached from another rough road which runs past the volcanoes about 10km S.
**CLIMB**   Licancabur can be climbed from any direction but  try to climb by a lava rib where the ground is  surprisingly stable. Descend on the loose ash between ribs.
**OTHER PEAKS**   The easy neighbouring peak of **Sairecabur 5971m, F** is best climbed from the col between it and Licancabur by the S slopes. **Juriques 5704m, F** is easiest to reach from the SW but could also be climbed from the Lag. Verde.
**BEST  MAP**   ChIGM  SF-19-11-12,  'Calama',  1:250,000  is  adequate.  1:50,000  maps  not available.

# PUNA DE ATACAMA

## INTRODUCTION

The Puna de Atacama is a high plateau mostly over 4000m above sea level and over 200 miles wide. This is undoubtedly the bleakest and most remote part of the Andes. The Puna extends from southern Bolivia and northern Chile into NW Argentina. Rainfall is very low and there are many peaks over 6000m with little or no permanent snow on them. Peaks and roads for the whole Puna are shown on map 39

The area has the greatest concentration of high peaks in the Andes with over 30 principal 6000m summits and six of the ten highest peaks. Over the last few decades there have been various reports that Ojos del Salado and/or Pissis was higher than Aconcagua, with Ojos once being surveyed at 7104m. These reports have never been substantiated. Recent surveys to indicate that Pissis is higher than Ojos del Salado.

There are undoubtedly many peaks of over 5000m not yet climbed and there may even be a few 6000m peaks awaiting first ascents. Some of the highest summits were climbed at the time of the Inca empire, over 400 years ago. Remains and ruins (as well as treasure and sacrifice victims) have been found on numerous peaks and have given rise to the unusual sport or science of high altitude archaeology. To date the highest ruins which have been found are the two small huts just under the summit of Llullaillaco (6739m). These are also the highest ruins that have been excavated by archaeologists. See page 150 for more details.

The peaks are described in four areas. Firstly the peaks of the NW with access usually from Calama. Secondly the peaks of the NE with access from Salta, thirdly the peaks of the SW around Ojos del Salado with access from Copiapó and finally the peaks of the SE around Pissis and Bonete with access from Catamarca in Argentina.

The bleak and inhospitable surroundings and constant desolate wind are not to everyone's taste, but the immense views and the wonderful clarity of the air leave a deep impression on everyone who visits the Puna.

## GETTING THERE

Many mountains can be approached from either Chile or Argentina. For Chilean approaches fly out to Santiago and then either fly or take the bus to one of the two main centres, Calama (described above in the Cordillera Occidental chapter) or Copiapó, described below. For the Argentine side of the mountains fly out to Buenos Aires then on to Salta for Chañi, Libertador and Llullaillaco. To reach the Ojos del Salado and Pissis regions from Argentina fly from Buenos Aires to either Catamarca or La Rioja. See the High Andes chapter for details of flights to Santiago and Buenos Aires from Europe the USA and Australia.

## SEASON

Because of the dry nature of the terrain climbs can be made at any time of year in most of the Puna, though the winter months of May to September are reckoned to be best for the Salta ranges, There are lots of different opinions about when to climb in the area around Ojos del Salado and Pissis. The wetter winter means a lower snowline but difficulties due to the extreme cold. The summer is drier and possibly too hot lower down. The spring months of October to December are probably the best on balance.

## CLIMBING CONDITIONS

Almost without exception the peaks are of volcanic origin and are technically easy ascents over scree and snow slopes. Crampons will only occasionally be needed for the highest peaks. The problems of an ascent are usually confined to the extreme remoteness and lack of water and the constant cold and windy conditions. These hazards should not be underestimated.

Water (or snow) is generally more easy to obtain on the Argentine side of the range.

## OTHER GUIDE BOOKS   none known

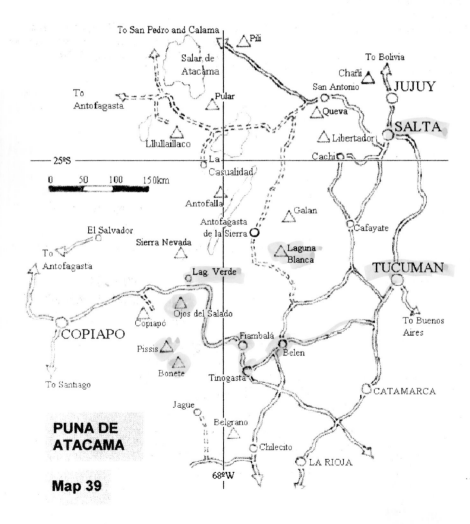

# Co. de PILI  6046m          Map 40          4 days    F

The highest point on the vast plateau E of the Salar de Atacama, also known as Acaramachi. Pili is a fine conical volcano known to have had Inca ascents. The first ascensionists found Indian gold and silver statuettes, textiles, feathers and hair.

**ACCESS**    From Calama in Chile via San Pedro and the picturesque oasis village of Toconao (2500m) (PT). Approaching along the old road by 4WD would be easiest. The old road over to Salta passes about 20km SW of Pili, but buses now go via the new road further S passing no nearer than 40km from Pili.

**CLIMB**    No details but easy.

**OTHER PEAKS**  To the SW and nearer the old road  lies  **V. Lascar 5641m, F.** This is one of the most active volcanoes in the Andes. There are many other high and easily climbed volcanoes in the area including **Aguas Calientes 5924m, Chilliques 5778m** and **Tumisa 5658m.**

**BEST MAP**  ChIGM sheet 2300-6700 'Toconao' 1:250,000

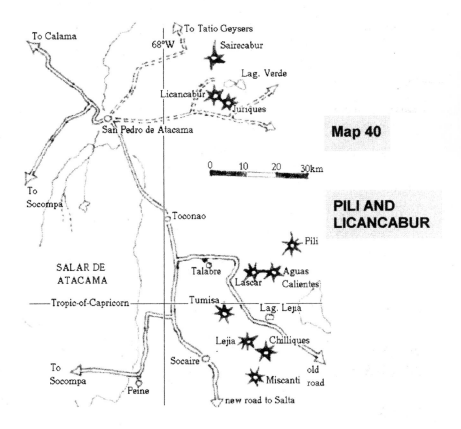

# V. SOCOMPA 6031m

| | | | |
|---|---|---|---|
| **V. SOCOMPA** 6031m | Map 41 | 4 days | F |
| **Co. SALIN** 6029m | Map 41 | 6 days | N/K |
| **Co. PULAR** 6225m | Map 41 | 6 days | F |
| **Co. ARACAR** 6080m | Map 41 | 7 days | F |

A group of high volcanoes lying SE of the Salar de Atacama. All have produced evidence of Inca ascents. Salin and Socompa lie on the Chile - Argentina border, Pular, with an Inca altar on the summit is entirely in Chile and Aracar lies inside Argentina. Access to Socompa is reasonable, but the others are very remote. Pular is Atacameñan for 'eyebrow'.

**ACCESS** Very difficult without private transport. Goods trains still run to Estacion Socompa on the Antofagasta - Salta line from both ends, but services can be erratic. The Chileans do not officially allow passengers on these trains, the Argentineans do. It is a long journey and, apart from V. Socompa, still leaves a long way to go to get to the base of the mountains. With private 4WD transport a roadhead for most peaks could be reached in a day from Calama, or 2 days from Salta in Argentina.

**CLIMBS** V. Socompa is an easy ascent by the S slopes form Estacion Socompa. Pular and Salin are probably best climbed from Estacion Socompa, approaching (may be possible with good 4WD) round the E side of V. Socompa. Aracar may be easier to reach from the railway to the S at Taca Taca. Ascents are all easy and all peaks have very little or no snow on them in a normal year.

**BEST MAP** ChIGM sheet 2400-6715 'Sierra Almeida' 1:250,000 covers all the peaks though Aracar is only partly shown.

**LLULLAILLACO AREA**

**Map 41**

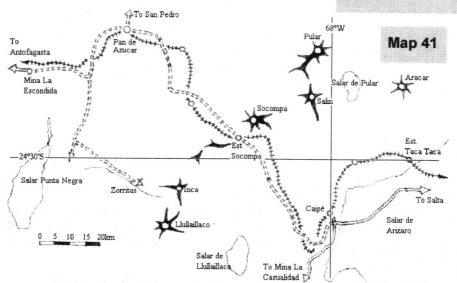

# V. LLULLAILLACO 6739m   Map 41          5 days    F

Llullaillaco is the mountain with the highest archaeological ruins in the world on the summit. The supposed first ascensionists, a Polish party in 1952 were reported to be very surprised to find ruined walls and houses on the summit area. The mountain was climbed at the time of the Inca empire for religious purposes, see appendix for further details. Llullaillaco, the 8th highest Andean peak, is also an active volcano with eruptions reported from the last century. The name means 'water of memory', a rather haunting name for such a remote desert peak.

**ACCESS** See under Socompa for details of the railway to Estacion Socompa. This still leaves 2-3d. walking across the desert to V. Llullaillaco. From the Chilean side, either from Antofagasta or from Calama via San Pedro, it is possible with a 4WD to go all the way to Q. de Las Zorritas (4200m) NW of the mountain where there is running water. To get to Zorritas drive to the change in direction in the road halfway between La Escondida and Pan de Azucar. From here head S to the N end of Salar Punta Negra then look for the track heading E and up to Zorritas. This area has many water pumps (no water) and dead end roads which make finding the right track difficult. Access may also be possible from the area of the La Casualidad mine in Argentina, 50km SE.

**CLIMB** By the N, NW or NE sides several routes possible. The small glacier (no crevasses) R of the obvious lava flow on the NW flank is probably the most interesting line. The base of this can be reached up Q. de Las Zorritas or more steeply, up Q. Culpeo. From Argentina the E side is easy to ascend but harder to approach.

**OTHER PEAKS**
15km to the N of Llullaillaco **Co. Inca 5540m, F** can also be climbed from Zorritas.
**BEST MAP** ChIGM sheet 2430-6820 'Volcan Llullaillaco', 1:50,000

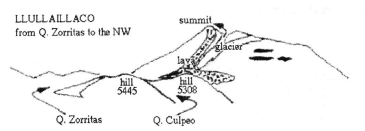

LLULLAILLACO from Q. Zorritas to the NW — summit, glacier, lava, hill 5445, hill 5308, Q. Zorritas, Q. Culpeo

# SALTA   The principal city of NW Argentina          1187m

Salta is a pleasant city in NW Argentina and a good base for trips into the northern Argentine Puna. There are several flights a day from Buenos Aires and many buses.

**SIGHTS** There are some nice colonial buildings around the centre of the city. Co. San Bernardo has good views of the city. Cable car or trail to summit. The Q. de Humahuaca lies beyond the smaller city of Jujuy, 80km N of Salta, and contains several important archaeological ruins from the time of the Incas, the best probably the fort of Pucará.

**FUEL** Petrol and kerosene from service stations
**MOUNTAIN INFO AND TRANSPORT** Try Puna Expediciones, Braquiquitos 399
**MOUNTAIN EQUIPMENT** Try the camping shop at La Rioja 995

**Map 42**    **SALTA AREA**

# No. QUEVA 6135m          Map 42          6 days    F

Also known as Quehuar, Pastos Grandes or Quironcollo. An Inca grave on the summit containing a mummy was dynamited by local treasure hunters.

**ACCESS** From Salta by train, bus or jeep to Olacapato (3900m) (facilities n/k).

**CLIMB** Easily by the N and NE slopes. No snow.

**OTHER PEAKS** Nearer Salta **No. Acay 5950m, F** is sometimes quoted as being over 6000m. Climb easily from the road at Encrucijada (3500m) to the NE.

**BEST MAP** AIGM sheet n/k.

## No. de CHAÑI 6060m          Map 42          5 days     F

Chañi lies about 100km N of Salta, near the small city of Jujuy. It is one of many peaks in NW
Argentina that has Inca ruins on the summit.
**ACCESS**   From Salta travel via Jujuy to the settlement at Leon (1622m) (PT). From here walk
up the valley to reach the E side of Chañi. 2-3d.
**CLIMB**   By the E side. Easy, mostly rock.
**BEST MAP**   AIGM sheet n/k.

## Co. LIBERTADOR 6380m       Map 42          6 days     F
## Co. QUEMADO 6120m          Map 42          6 days  N/K

Libertador is also known as San Martin after the liberator of Argentina. It is the highest point of
the Nevados de Cachi. Early sources give the height as 6720m, almost certainly a mistake.
**ACCESS**   From Salta to the village of Cachi. (2270m)(PT).  Walk up the canyon to the NW
towards the S face of the mountain. For Quemado go N out of Cachi to Pueblo Viejo and walk in
up the valley to the SE flank of the mountain.
**CLIMBS**   Climb Libertador by the S side - some snow. Climb Quemado from the SE.
**OTHER PEAKS**   To the N of Libertador are a number of other high summits including **Cienaga
6030m**, also known as Palermo, which can be climbed from Pueblo Viejo by its E flank.
**BEST MAP**   AIGM sheet n/k.

## V. ANTOFALLA 6440m         Map 39          10 days    F

Antofalla, an active volcano, is one of the remotest 6000m peaks in the Andes, located about
80km NW of Antofagasta de la Sierra. Many sources quote a height of only 6100m.
**ACCESS**    The best possibilities are probably from the remote village of Antofagasta de la
Sierra or from the Mina La Casualidad 60km to the NW of the peak. Both of these can be
reached from San Antonio de los Cobres on the Salta - Calama road. It is easier to get to
Antofagsta de la Sierra from the town of Belen to the S in Catamarca province (occasional PT).
**CLIMB**   No information but easy.
**BEST MAP**   AIGM sheet n/k.

## Co. GALAN 5912m            Map 39          6 days     F
## Sa. LAGUNA BLANCA 5900m    Map 39          6 days  N/K

Galan lies 40km E of Antofagasta de la Sierra. The peak known as Laguna Blanca lies about
50km SE. There is some doubt about the height of both peaks, the above figures are from the
latest Argentine surveys. Laguna Blanca is sometimes quoted as 6195m and Galan has been
quoted at 6116m but also at only 5500m.
**ACCESS**   As for Antofalla then by 4WD from Antofagasta de la Sierra to the peaks.
**CLIMBS**   No information but both are likely to be easy.
**BEST MAP**   AIGM sheet n/k.

# Co. SIERRA NEVADA 6127m    Map 43    8 days  N/K
# Cos. COLORADOS 6080m    Map 43    8 days  N/K
# Co. EL CONDOR 6108m    Map 43    8 days  N/K

Three very remote peaks which lie between 30 and 80km N of the Paso de San Francisco. There are no recorded ascents of any of these peaks and information is very scarce. The names are all Spanish. Sierra Nevada means snowy mountains, Cerros Colorados means red hills  and Cerro El Condor is peak of the condor. El Condor is also known as V. Sarmiento, Colorados is also known as Vallecitos.

**ACCESS** Sierra Nevada lies on the border 25km E of the Rio Juncalito. There is a track from the Chilean mining town of El Salvador to thermals here, probably the best approach. The Colorados peaks are probably also best approached from Juncalito or directly from  the W. El Condor is probably best approached from the Lag. Verde (see under Ojos) which lies 30km due S. No information is available about the state of tracks in this area. All approaches will be long and require a 4WD!

**CLIMBS** No information but probably all easy.

**BEST   MAP**   ChIGM sheet  2600-6730  'Laguna Verde'  1:250,000

**Map 43**

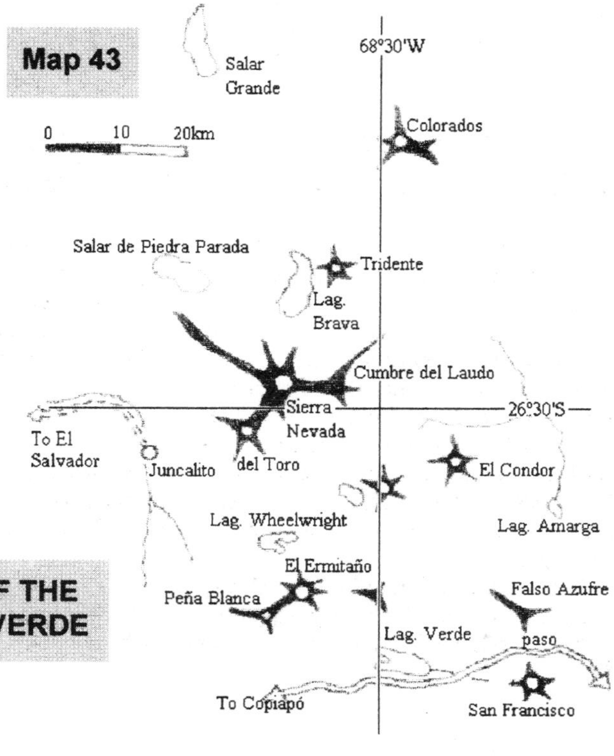

Salar Grande

68°30'W

0    10    20km

Colorados

Salar de Piedra Parada

Tridente

Lag. Brava

Cumbre del Laudo

Sierra — 26°30'S —

Nevada

To El Salvador

Juncalito    del Toro

El Condor

Lag. Wheelwright

Lag. Amarga

El Ermitaño

**NORTH OF THE LAGUNA VERDE**

Peña Blanca

Falso Azufre

Lag. Verde    paso

To Copiapó

San Francisco

# Co. EL ERMITAÑO 6187m       Map 44       3 days       F
# Cos. PEÑA BLANCA 6030m       Map 44       3 days       F

El Ermitaño and Peña Blanca are two neighbouring peaks to the N of the road to the San Francisco pass which are sometimes climbed as a warm up before an ascent of Ojos del Salado. Ermitaño means the hermit, Peña Blanca means the white stone.
**ACCESS**   As for the base area of Ojos del Salado to the ruined hosteria.
**CLIMB**   The peaks, which lie about 15km N of the road can be climbed easily by S side from near the ruined hosteria. Normally no snow.
**BEST MAP**   ChIGM sheet 2645-6830, 'Rio Peñas Blancas' 1:50,000


# COPIAPÓ    Main access town for the Chilean Puna        370m

A small city in a fruit growing region and the most important access town for the Chilean side of the Puna. Flights daily from Santiago or buses day and night which take about 12h.
**MOUNTAIN TRANSPORT, INFO AND EQUIPMENT**   There is a list of 4WD drivers kept at the tourist office or try the car hire agencies for a jeep with driver (Hertz at Copayapu 173) or the adventure travel company at Rodriguez 771.
**FOOD AND FUEL**   Plenty places in town.


# Co. COPIAPÓ 6080m        Map 44       5 days       F
# Co. TRES QUEBRADAS 6250m       Map 44       7 days       F

Co. Copiapó, an active volcano, is another of the high peaks in this area with ruins near the summit. Ruins including terraces, retaining walls, fireplaces and altars have been discovered. Co. Tres Quebradas is also known as Co. de Los Patos. No snow or glaciers on these peaks.
**ACCESS**   For both peaks the best access is from the N (Chilean side). A track runs S from the main Copiapó - Paso San Francisco road (see Ojos). This leaves the road at the E side of Salar de Maricunga and goes up the Q. Vega Redonda to  the mine of Proyecto Marte (c.4200m). Hitching is apparently easy to this area. The track is marked as continuing on to Lag. del Negro Francisco which is S of Co. Copiapó but state is n/k.
**COPIAPÓ CLIMB**   Copiapó is an easy ascent from the mine Proyecto Marte to the E.
**TRES QUEBRADAS CLIMB**   The W summit is 5980m and lies on the Chilean border. The peak can be climbed from the Proyecto Marte mine (4WD may get closer) in several days over easy W slopes.
**BEST MAP**   ChIGM sheet SG-19-14 'Copiapó' 1:250,000 shows the summit of Co. Copiapó but not the approach. The western approaches to both peaks are shown on ChIGM sheet 2600-6815 'Copiapó' 1:500,000. For Tres Quebradas the Argentine map AIGM 1:250,000 sheet n/k.

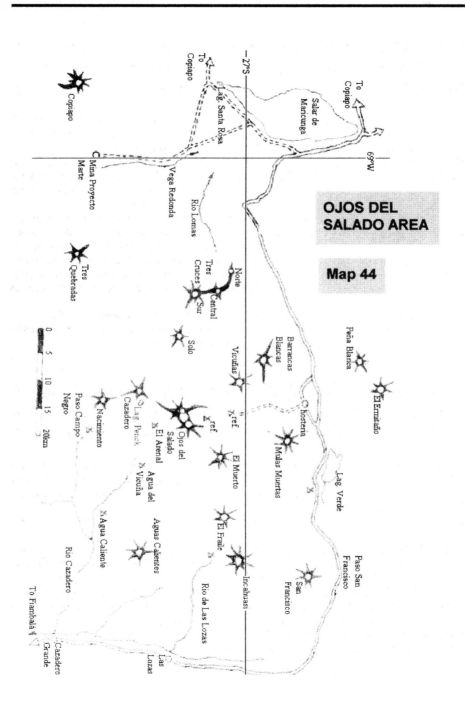

OJOS DEL
SALADO AREA

Map 44

## Nos. TRES CRUCES Sur 6749m    Map 44    6 days    F
## Nos. TRES CRUCES Central 6629m  Map 44    6 days    F
## Co. SOLO 6190m                  Map 44    5 days    F

The Tres Cruces massif is one of the highest in the Andes, with two major 6000m summits. It has more snow and ice than other peaks in the area and the above heights are probably correct (the peaks are often quoted around 6330m). Tres Cruces is Spanish for three crosses.
**ACCESS** Much easier from the Chilean side. From Copiapó take the San Francisco pass road until about 15-20km E of Lag. Santa Rosa then continue on rough track S of Rio Lomas. When this track turns N leave it and head E and drive up sandy fan towards T.C. Sur to a dry base camp at 4600m. For Solo approach via the San Francisco road to the N side of the peak.
**TRES CRUCES CLIMBS** Establish a second camp at 5300-5500m below the col between Sur and Central. **Tres Cruces Norte 6030m** can be climbed from here by easy E slopes in one day. For the two main summits place another camp beside the lake at 5940m in the crater 1km W of 6008m col. From here climb Central by the S glacier or SW scree slopes, 1d. For Sur climb towards 6008m col but head S up a rib before reaching it. Then climb up snow fields and a gully to the shoulder at 6440m (poss. high camp). Scramble up blocks and a short wall on W slopes to the summit.
**SOLO CLIMB** Solo is a very sandy climb - swim up the slopes from a camp to the N.
**BEST MAP** ChIGM sheet 2700-6845 'Macizo Tres Cruces'. Sheets 2645-6845, and 2645-6830 both at 1:50,000 show the road and would be useful for the approach.

## Cos. BARRANCAS BLANCAS 6119m  Map 44  3 days  F
## Co. VICUÑAS 6067m            Map 44    3 days N/K
## No. EL MUERTO 6476m          Map 44    3 days  F

These three peaks lie S of the road to the Paso San Francisco and are outlying peaks of the Ojos del Salado massif. All are easy ascents, and for Puna peaks all are climbed relatively frequently as warm up peaks for Ojos del Salado. El Muerto is Spanish for 'the dead one', the Vicuña is a wild relative of the llama.
**ACCESS** As for Ojos del Salado to either the base area, the lower refugio or El Arenal on the Argentine side.
**EL MUERTO CLIMB** From between the two refugios on Ojos, traverse E and set up a camp in the col between Ojos and El Muerto. Climb easily over scree and snow slopes to the summit. El Muerto can also be climbed from the El Arenal area in Argentina.
**OTHER CLIMBS** Barrancas Blancas is best climbed from the old hosteria (4500m) by its N slopes or E ridge, probably with an intermediate camp. Vicuñas is probably best climbed by its S or SE slopes from the refugio at 5200m on the N slopes of Ojos.
**BEST MAPS** ChIGM sheet 2645-6830, 'Rio Peñas Blancas' 1:50,000 shows Barrancas Blancas. ChIGM sheet 2600-6815 'Copiapó' 1:500,000 shows all four peaks.

# No. OJOS DEL SALADO 6864m    Map 44     6 days   F/PD

Ojos del Salado is the highest mountain in Chile and also the highest active volcano in the world, with fumaroles in the crater SW of the summit. Ojos del Salado was for a long time thought to be the second highest peak in the Andes, though recent surveys appear to indicate that Pissis is higher. Both peaks have also occasionally been surveyed higher than Aconcagua.

The name is often wrongly translated as 'Eyes of the Salt Plain'. Ojo is Spanish for 'source' and Salado is the name given to numerous salt rivers in the area so a better translation is 'Source of the Salt River'

Ojos del Salado is easier to approach from the Chilean side because the access is easier and there are also a couple of refugios. The climb itself is easier from the Argentine side. There are two tops of very similar height.

**CHILEAN ACCESS**  Access to the Chilean side is reasonably easy for a Puna peak. Official permission will be needed to get through the police check point at Maricunga. (from DINAF, Calle Bandera 53 in Santiago - fax 6971909). The road from Copiapó to Tinogasta over the Paso San Francisco (4720m) passes about 20km N of Ojos del Salado. 4WD is recommended but not essential for this road. At the E end of Lag. Verde (4300m) is the Arroyo Agua Dulce which is the only source of drinkable water for many miles and could be used as a base camp while acclimatising for Ojos and the surrounding peaks. A tourist bus does this trip once a week in summer between Argentina and Copiapó. There is a 4WD track up the N side of the mountain, starting about 5km W of the Lag. Verde at the ruined hosteria. Well acclimatised parties can drive all the way to the lower refugio (no facilities) at 5200m and possibly still reach the higher one (no facilities) at 5750m.

**ARGENTINE ACCESS**  Access to the Argentine side of the mountain starts from the village of Fiambalá in the province of Catamarca. The approach walk is longer than from the Chilean side but there is more fresh water and it is usually possible to arrange mules. The trail head is at Cazadero Grande (3600m) in the Valle de Chaschuil where there is an arrieros camp in summer. Follow the Rio Cazadero W to major junction of streams, turn N and follow this river for to its source at Agua Caliente (4300m), 1½d. Another day gets you to Agua del Vicuña at 4950m. This is as far as mules can go. Allow 1-2 more days to reach a camp on a large plain known as El Arenal (5500m) on SE side of Ojos.

**CHILEAN CLIMB**  The grade of PD is justified only by the summit rock buttress, c. 60m, III. From the refugios on the Chilean side some variation is possible but climb up valleys which lie S and SE to reach the NW slopes and a groove-cum-gully which leads to a notch in the narrow N ridge. Climb to the summit on this ridge, some fixed ropes.

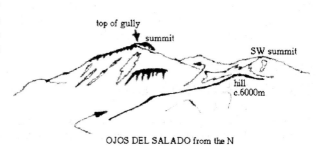

OJOS DEL SALADO from the N

**ARGENTINE CLIMB** From the 5500m camp on the Argentine side some variation is possible but climb up the valley to the NW (high camp at 5900m usual) then the slopes above to the summit marked by a bronze pyramid. Easier than Chilean ascent.

**OTHER PEAKS** The western top about 2km away is 6720m.

**BEST MAP** ChIGM 2600-6815 'Copiapó' 1:500,000, shows the Chilean side of the border only (the height of 5893m is definitely a misprint). The 1:50,000 sheet is not available at present. ChIGM sheet 2645-6815, 'Paso San Francisco' 1:50,000, shows the Lag. Verde. For Argentine side AIGM 1:250,000 sheets 2769-II and 2769-IV, watch out for 200m contours!

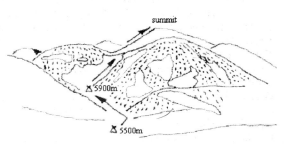

OJOS DEL SALADO from the SE

# No. de INCAHUASI 6621m     Map 44     5 days   F
# No. de SAN FRANCISCO 6020m   Map 44     3 days   F
# No. EL FRAILE 6060m     Map 44     5 days   N/K

The little known Incahuasi is one of the highest peaks in the Andes. Named after the Inca ruin discovered on the summit in 1913. There is a large snow filled crater to the S of the summit. Incahuasi means 'house of the Inca'. El Fraile is Spanish for friar. San Francisco is St. Francis.

**CHILEAN ACCESS** As for Ojos del Salado along the Paso San Francisco road to a base camp at the E end of Lag. Verde. All three peaks can be climbed from here - allow about 2 days each. It may be possible to get closer in a 4WD.

**ARGENTINE ACCESS** For the Argentine side approach by the Rio de Las Lozas to the S side of mountains, little or no water, 2-3d. This area can also be reached from El Arenal in 2d.

**CLIMBS** Incahuasi can be climbed easily by the NW slopes or by the S side from Argentina. San Francisco can be climbed most easily by the N slopes from the pass (4800). Little or no snow on either peak. El Fraile is likely to be an easy climb too.

**BEST MAP** ChIGM sheet 2600-6815 'Copiapó' 1:500,000. ChIGM sheet 2645-6815, 'Paso San Francisco' 1:50,000, shows the Lag. Verde and would be useful for the approach. For Argentine side AIGM 1:250,000 sheets as for Ojos.

# Co. CAZADERO 6658m     Map 44     9 days   F
# Co. NACIMIENTO 6490m     Map 44     9 days   F

Cazadero is a huge and little known peak lying about 10km S of Ojos del Salado. It is also known as Walter Penck after the first ascenscionist. Nacimiento is S of Cazadero and marked incorrectly as Co. Bayo on Argentine map. Cazadero means the hunter, Nacimiento means birth (i.e. source of a river).

**ACCESS** As for Ojos del Salado to the river junction then follow the main valley W towards Campo Negro pass but before reaching this turn N to establish base camp(s) on the E side of the peaks at c.5200m. Cazadero can also be reached by following Ojos access to El Arenal then heading W to Lag. Penck.

**CAZADERO CLIMB** From Lag. Penck an easy ascent via the col between this peak and Co. A.T.A. to the N then continue up rough N slopes. A higher camp may be desirable. 1-1½d.

**NACIMIENTO CLIMB** An easy climb by the E slopes over a subsidiary top, on a mixture of scree and snow. 1d.

**BEST MAP** AIGM 1:250,000 sheets as for Ojos.

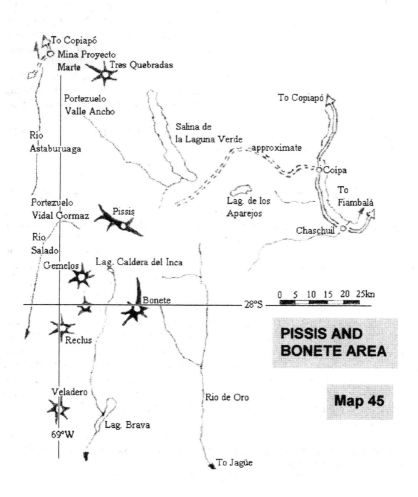

# MONTE PISSIS  6882m          Map 45          9 days          F

Pissis has recently been re-surveyed and there seems to be some good evidence that at 6882m it is higher than Ojos del Salado (recent surveys 6864m). Five summits have been reported on the extensive summit plateau, the highest is the W summit, but the NE is just lower. Though it has more snow and ice than other peaks in the area Pissis is an easy ascent. Access is difficult but quicker from Chile - this is technically illegal. The mountain is named after a French scientist.
**ARGENTINE ACCESS**  Drive by 4WD from Fiambalá and Valle de Chascuil, turning off the main road at Coipa and passing Lag. de Los Aparejos and the S end of the Salina de la Laguna Verde to a camp (5300m) at the bottom of the main glacier on the N side of Pissis. About 60km, poor tracks and cross country. Access is also possible from Jagüe to the S (see under Bonete).
**CHILEAN ACCESS**  This will probably prove to be the quickest and cheapest but it may be hard to find a willing driver. From Copiapó via the Mina Proyecto Marte (hitching on mine vehicles possible) then cross the border (illegal) at Port. de Valle Ancho Norte and then drive E for 50km to the base camp by the N glacier. With transport only to the border this approach would be a 2-3d walk.
**CLIMB**  Several higher camps will be necessary. The normal route is on the N side. Follow scree slopes to the E of the large glacier then traverse around or over lower summits E of the main summit to reach the highest W peak. If penitentes are not bad the glacier can be taken direct to this summit, 30-40°.
For the S side establish a camp by lakes at 5250m. Then either climb the steep S slopes directly or cross pass between Pissis and point 6038m and join NW route.
**BEST MAP**  AIGM sheet 2769-III, 'Fiambalá, 1:250,000.

# Co. BONETE  6759m          Map 45          9 days          F

Bonete is one of the highest peaks in the Andes. The peak is a very easy ascent but access is difficult. The summit massif is reported to be complex with three tops, the S top is highest.
This peak was for many years marked as Bonete Chico (Little Bonete) on Argentine maps, giving rise to much confusion because a smaller peak to the N was labelled Bonete Grande. To eliminate further confusion the name Bonete is used here and the adjective Chico is dropped.
**ACCESS**  Bonete can be approached either from the Valle de Chaschuil (as for Pissis, but a long walk at the end) or from the S from the village of Jagüe follow the road to Boca de Quebrada (16km). From here there is a 60km walk (mules may be possible) up the Rio Bonete, Rio de Oro then Q. Peña Negra to a camp at 5000m on S side of mountain. Water available on this route. Another possibility is a 4WD track which goes from Jagüe W to Salar de Leoncito then N past Lag. Brava and up the Veladero valley to Lag. Caldera del Inca at the base of the NW slopes at 5100m (very rough driving - convoy recommended). This valley would also give access to the S side of Pissis. This flank of Bonete can also be approached (illegally) from Chile via the Rio Astaburuaga (plenty water) and over the border by the Port. Vidal Gormaz. 1d walk if no driver is willing to cross the border.
**CLIMB**  Routes on the E or SE side are straightforward, sand, scree and possibly some snow. For the NW side walk around S side of the Caldera del Inca to the Lagoon at 5900m then follow NE ridge past two false summits to the highest top.
**BEST MAP**  AIGM sheet 2796 III 'Fiambalá and 2969-II 'Tinogasta', 1:250,000.

# VELADERO 6436m
# RECLUS 6320m
# LOS GEMELOS 6159m

| | |
|---|---|
| Map 45 | 9 days F |
| Map 45 | 9 days F |
| Map 45 | 9 days F |

These three peaks lie S and W of Bonete in the Sierra del Veladero and are all remote summits There are ruins on the summit of Reclus. The names used here are taken from Johan Rheinhard's excellent article on the highest peaks in the Andes (South American Explorer # 26). There is still some confusion about names and heights in this area. In particular the name Veladero seems to have been used for other peaks in the area. Los Gemelos is Spanish for the twins.
**ACCESS**  The only realistic way into this area is from Jagüe, with a 4WD by the route described under Bonete to reach the Veladero valley.
**CLIMBS**    Little information but all have been climbed and all are easy. There are some small glaciers and penitente fields on all three peaks.
**BEST MAP**  AIGM 1:250,000 sheet 2969-II 'Tinogasta'. Sheet 2969-I 'Pastillos' may be useful for access to this area.

# Co. Gral. BELGRANO 6250m    Map 46    3 days    F

Belgrano, also known as La Mejicana or Famatina, is the highest point of the Nevados de Famatina range, an isolated spur of the southern Puna. Named after the famous Argentine general.
**ACCESS**  From  La Rioja by bus to the town of Chilecito (1074m). Then through the small village of Famatina (PT) to the abandoned Mejicana mine at 4375m on the E slopes of the mountain range.
**CLIMB**    From  Mejicana by  the  E slopes, easy, some small snowfields. 2d.
**OTHER PEAKS** To the N the lower summit of **Negro Overo 6000m, F** has ruins on the summit.
**BEST MAP**    AIGM 1:250,000 sheet n/k.

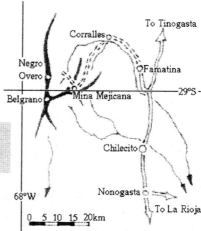

**NEVADOS DE FAMATINA**

**Map 46**

# THE HIGH ANDES

## INTRODUCTION
This section covers the Andes from 29°S to 35°S and includes some of the highest peaks in the Andes. The area is dominated by three high peaks - Tupungato, Mercedario and the highest in the Andes, Aconcagua. South of 35°S there is a sharp transition to lower peaks. This part of the Andean chain is much narrower and the mountains in many places form a single distinct chain. There are few volcanoes in the area and almost all mountains are of folded origin.

In general the area is one of the best known in the Andes, though it is very little explored by European and North American mountaineers. Several of the lower and more accessible ranges, notably the Loma Larga and Vallecitos groups offer numerous alpine peaks with classic ridges and ice-faces. These ranges have been well explored by local Chilean and Argentine mountaineers, though many good lines will still be found. Away from these areas are many unspoilt and rarely climbed peaks and probably still some unclimbed 5000'ers. Aconcagua is the only really busy peak in the area.

Despite being near some of the biggest Andean cities the three highest peaks all have long approach marches. The low altitude of the base cities can lead to acclimatisation problems.

The area is probably the poorest in the Andes for seeing wildlife and traditional culture. It is on the other hand one of the easiest from which to organise an expedition as both Chile and Argentina are relatively modern, well organised and relaxing countries in which to travel.

## GETTING THERE
The best option for most of this area is to fly to the Argentine capital Buenos Aires and then on to Mendoza with an internal flight or to take an international flight direct to Santiago, the capital of Chile. There are direct flights to both cities from most European capitals, including London, Paris, Madrid, Frankfurt and Amsterdam. Aerolineas Argentinas offer very good deals on internal flights if you fly to Argentina with them. There are daily flights from Miami to Santiago and Buenos Aires as well as less frequent flights from New York, Toronto and Los Angeles to Buenos Aires. There is also a weekly Aerolineas flight from Sydney to Buenos Aires.

Flying to San Juan from Buenos Aires may be a better option for Mercedario and the northernmost peaks. From Chile the three northernmost peaks are best approached from the city of La Serena - daily flights from Santiago or a comfortable 8 hour bus journey.

## SEASON
December to March is the climbing season in this part of the Andes. At this time of year the climate is in general very dry and stable - particularly so in the far N of this area, bordering the Puna. Storms lasting a few days occur once a month or so in summer and these can bring heavy snowfalls as low as 4000m. Persistent strong winds are common all year at altitude and Aconcagua has a particularly bad reputation. Mountains on the Argentine side are drier than those in Chile. Obtaining water is not normally a problem.

## CLIMBING CONDITIONS
In the far N expect conditions resembling those found in the Puna - dry approaches and high snowlines. Around Santiago and Mendoza climbing is about as similar to the Alps as it gets in the Andes - long sunny days can lead to soft snow in the afternoons, but cold nights usually lead

to a re-freeze. Penitentes are common on N slopes. Snow lines are about 5500m in the N of the area, dropping to about 4500m in the mountains around Santiago, with some bigger glaciers as low as 4000m. Glaciers tend to be biggest on the S and E slopes. Many N slopes, such as the normal route on Aconcagua, are normally free of snow. River crossings can be a major hazard on the approaches to many peaks in this area - using mules may be necessary for this reason alone. On all but the most popular peaks it may be hard to obtain mules on the spot as there are fewer people living off the land than there are in Peru and Bolivia.

**OTHER GUIDE BOOKS**
Aconcagua, R. J. Secor, The Mountaineers.
Backpacking in Chile and Argentina., Bradt Publications.

# Co. DEL TORO 6380m               Map 47        10 days    F

Toro is the highest of the three 6000m peaks near the Agua Negra pass. This area is a transitional area between the Puna and the High Andes of the Santiago - Mendoza area. All three peaks are easiest to approach from Chile. A mummified corpse, with only the top of skull showing was found on the first modern ascent of Toro in 1964. The corpse was of a young man, wearing grey trousers, red cap and poncho. There was a wound to the back of his neck, so speculation is that he was a sacrifice victim. Co. Del Toro is Spanish for 'peak of the bull'.
**ACCESS**    From the Chilean city of Vallenar (1d on bus from Santiago) through Alto del Carmen (PT) then up the river which becomes the Rio del Transito then the Rio Conay on tracks for a further 60km to the place called Conay, (1600m) (facilities n/k). From here follow the Rio Valeriano to a base camp at c.4000m on the NW side of the mountain. Much of this may be driveable in a 4WD. Access is probably also possible, but less practical, from Rodeo in Argentina to Baños de San Crispin. This will be a long and complicated 4WD approach.
**CLIMB**  Normally by W side.
**BEST MAP**  ChIGM  sheet SH-19-10 1:250,000.

# Co. LAS TORTOLAS 6332m          Map 47        5 days     F
# Co. DE OLIVARES  6252m           Map 47        5 days  N/K

Access is easiest from the coastal resort city of La Serena in Chile, but is also possible from Argentina via San Juan and Rodeo. In Spanish tortolas are doves, olivares are olive groves.
**ACCESS**    From the city of La Serena drive through Vicuña and towards the Paso de Agua Negra. Infrequent buses go through the pass in summer (La Serena - La Rioja service). For Tortolas turn off up the Rio del Toro towards the mining area of Las Hediondas (c.3400m) on the W side of the mountains (condition of tracks n/k). For Olivares continue further up the main valley until W of the peak.
**TORTOLAS CLIMB**  Has been climbed by the SW slopes, some snowfields near summit.
**OLIVARES CLIMB**  Has been climbed by the W slope. Grade n/k but likely to be easy.
**BEST MAP**  ChIGM 1:250,000 sheet SH-19-10 and sheet SH-19-13-14

Photo: **Llullaillaco from Quebrada de las Zorritas, Puna de Atacama, Chile.** G. Biggar.

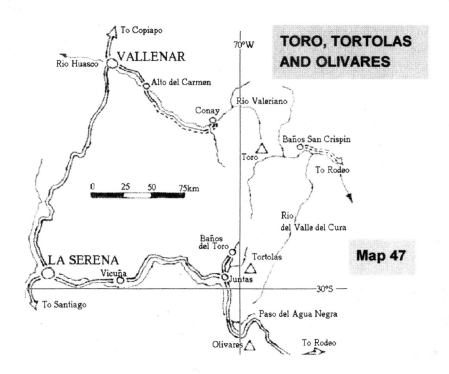

To Copiapo

70°W

**TORO, TORTOLAS AND OLIVARES**

Rio Huasco  VALLENAR

Alto del Carmen

Conay  Rio Valeriano

Toro

Baños San Crispin

To Rodeo

0   25   50   75km

Rio
del Valle del Cura

Baños
del Toro

**Map 47**

LA SERENA  Tortolas

Vicuña  Juntas

30°S

To Santiago

Paso del Agua Negra

Olivares  To Rodeo

# MENDOZA  A big city in W Argentina near Aconcagua  757m

Mendoza is one of the biggest and most prosperous cities in Argentina and the normal base for climbing Aconcagua. Permits need to be obtained here. It is a very pleasant clean and modern city with many tree lined avenues and pavement cafes. In the climbing season it is almost invariably very hot and dry.

**SIGHTS** There is nothing special to see in Mendoza but tours to the wineries can be enjoyable. A stroll round Parque San Martin to the W of the centre, with good views from Co. La Gloria is a good half day trip. Otherwise hang out in the pavement cafes on Sarmiento or San Martin.

**FOOD** There are many good quality supermarkets in the centre of town. There is a big one on the corner of Las Heras and Mendocinas and another almost opposite on Mitre that is even open on Sunday mornings!

**FUEL** Petrol and kerosene as usual from most petrol stations. Try for Camping Gas at the outdoor shop at Colon 733.

**MOUNTAIN TRANSPORT AND INFO** Try Andesport, Rufino Ortega 390, or Turismo Aymará at 9 de julio 983. For info on Aconcagua go to the Subsecretaria de Turismo (where you also buy permits).

**MOUNTAIN EQUIPMENT** Shop at Colon 733.

Photo: **The East side of Aconcagua from Casa de Piedra in the Vacas valley.** J. Biggar.

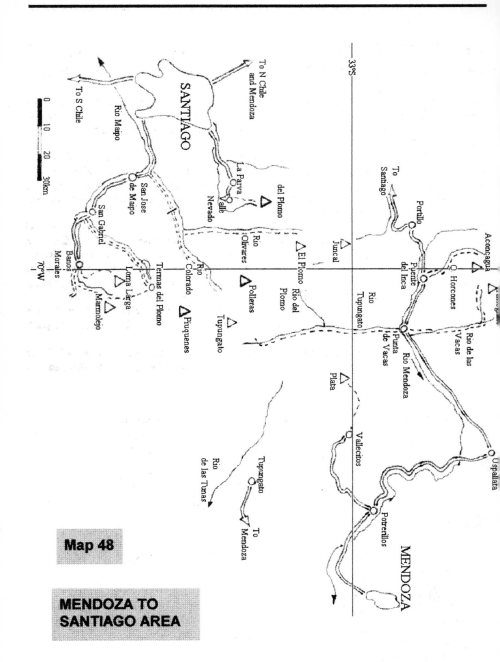

**Map 48**

**MENDOZA TO
SANTIAGO AREA**

# Co. MERCEDARIO 6770m    Map 49    8 days   F
# Co. LA RAMADA 6410m     Map 49    7 days  N/K

Mercedario, the 5th highest peak in the Andes is another of the high peaks which was probably climbed by the Incas. There are ruins at 5100m on the normal route up the E-NE ridge. With La Ramada it forms a huge glaciated cirque, nearly 15km across and facing NE. The native name for Mercedario is Lihue.

**ACCESS**    From the Argentine city of San Juan travel via Barreal (PT) then on  by 4WD past Casa Amarillo to the mining camp at Las Molles (2300m). Due to flooding in 1987 mules may be needed for the latter part of this route. From  Las Molles use mules to go SW up the side valley (Arroyo de la Laguna) on a deteriorating track to a base camp at 3900m. Access from Chile would be very difficult and illegal.

**MERCEDARIO CLIMB**  From the base camp head up slopes on RHS to avoid the ice fall and steep east face at the head of valley. Continue S to reach the camp known as Pircas Indias (Inca walls) (5200m). Then follow the reddish NE ridge with one further camp to reach summit easily.

**OTHER ROUTES**    From the same base camp the E face can be climbed directly via the Caballito glacier (50°). The 2000m S face of ice and snow can be climbed (in 2-3d.) from a camp in the upper Colorado valley. It is hard but much less serious than Aconcagua S face.

**LA RAMADA CLIMB** From Casa Amarillo on the Mercedario approach walk with mules SW up the Rio Colorado (big river crossings) to the NE slopes of the peak. Climb from here, grade n/k, but probably F or PD.

**OTHER PEAKS**  Several other points on the cirque can be climbed, mostly from the NE. These include the twin summits of **Polacos 6050m,** and the peaks of **Alma Negra 6120m,** and La

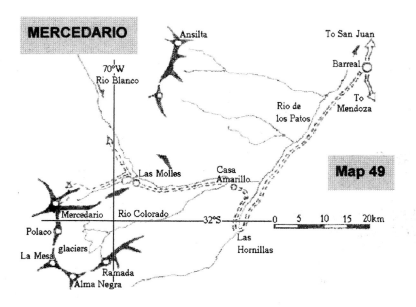

**Mesa 6200m.** Grades n/k. To the N of the Rio Blanco is the Cord. Ansilta. The highest point **Co. Ansilta 5885m**, is best approached from Calingasta on the W bank of the Rio de los Patos.

**BEST MAP**    Not known whether the AIGM 1:250,000 sheet is available for this area yet.

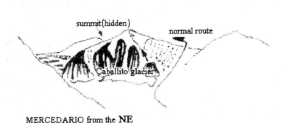

MERCEDARIO from the **NE**

# Co. ACONCAGUA 6959m    Map 50    10 days    F

Aconcagua is the highest peak in Argentina, in the Andes, in the Western and Southern Hemispheres and finally the highest in the world outside the Himalayan ranges. It also has a reputation as the highest peak in the world which is just a walk (i.e. no mountaineering skills are needed) but it should not be underestimated. The weather can be appalling, there are unstable boulder fields at over 6500m and there is often snow and ice requiring the use of an axe and crampons. More people die on this mountain than any other in South America, usually from altitude illness, exposure or both. While this is no doubt partly due to the large numbers attempting the mountain the lack of experience of many also leads to what is probably the highest death rate on any of the major Andean peaks.

The body of a guanaco was found on the summit ridge of Aconcagua in 1947 giving rise to speculation that the Incas may have climbed the mountain and giving the Cresta del Guanaco, which connects the N and S summits, its name. More recently the body of a boy was discovered on the flanks of the mountain by Argentine archaeologists. The name Aconcagua means 'stone sentinel' or 'white sentinel'.

Aconcagua has attracted a lot of stunt ascents. Bikes have been ridden on the summit, bears, cats and dogs have all been up to the top and motor bikes have been driven to 6500m. The national park authorities do not encourage such stunts any more.

Two routes are described in detail here 1. the normal route up the Horcones valley and the NW flank of the mountain and 2. the Polish glacier route up the Vacas valley and the Polish glacier on the NE side of the mountain. Traverses are possible between these routes once high on the mountain (5900-6300m) so in fact either approach can be used for either route.

Though ascents have been made in a matter of days the above time of 10 days should be regarded as a minimum safe time to attempt the normal route by a very fit party. There is a long approach and days will be needed for acclimatisation on the mountain. The Polish glacier will need a minimum of 12 days. Average times for most parties are 14 days for the normal route and 16 days for the Polish glacier.

**REGULATIONS**    The regulations change regularly. At present they are very simple. A permit needs to be obtained for each member of the expedition from the Subsecretaria de Turismo, San Martin 1143, Mendoza (open even on Sundays). This requires basic personal details and a fee of

$80 in 1995. The process takes only an hour at the most. The fee seems justified as the mountain is kept very clean and the base camps are staffed by rangers with radio communications.

**HORCONES ACCESS**    Go from Mendoza to Puente del Inca (2720m) (PT). Mules to carry gear to base camp can usually be arranged on the spot here. The natural bridge nearby is worth a look. There are cafes, hotels, bunkhouse and camping at Puente del Inca. The 30km walk to the Plaza de Mulas base camp usually takes two days with a camp at Confluencia (3350m). The trail actually starts at the ranger station at Lag. Horcones (4km W along main road then 2km N on a track). Start on the L side of river but cross by a bridge and go up the RHS. Cross the Lower Horcones river by the bridge at Confluencia (3350m). 12km beyond Confluencia there are numerous fords over the braided river for about 4km, then the Ibañez camp (3950m). 4km beyond this is the old Plaza de Mulas (4050m). Finally a steep climb leads to the new Plaza de Mulas (4250m) base. There is a hotel, restaurant and organised camping here.

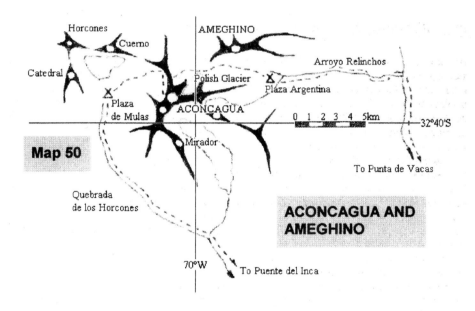

**VACAS ACCESS**    It is best to arrange mules in advance in Mendoza as far fewer climbers use the Vacas approach. Punta de Vacas has a couple of cafes. A good path starts on the W bank of the river. 5h to the first camp, ranger station and river crossing at Las Leñas. This serious crossing is much safer with mules but can be done (in the morning  only) without. The second day is normally to Casa de Piedra, where the Relinchos valley joins the main valley. 6h. The third day is usually up the Relinchos valley to base camp. The braided Vacas river is easy to cross at Casa de Piedra to gain the N bank of the Relinchos. Follow the Relinchos on a good but steep path, crossing twice (very narrow but  fast and quite deep). After a steep climb cross again and. follow the wide flat valley to the Plaza Argentina base camp in the moraines (4200m).

**NORMAL ROUTE**   Though there is no permanent snow and the route can be entirely over scree, an axe and crampons may be needed. All refugios are in a very poor state. From Plaza de Mulas follow the clear trail N and then E up vast scree slopes to Nido de Condores at 5350m. There are poor sites at 4900m and 5200m. 1d. From the Nido the summit and Canaleta can be seen at the top of the huge scree slope known as the Gran Acarreo. The route however continues E to gain the poorly defined NNW rib at 5950m - Berlin (Plantamura) camp. Continue up the LHS of ridge to White rocks camp at 6000m. Most parties go to the summit from either here or Berlin in one long day but higher camps are possible. From White rocks weave up the ridge to the Independencia ruin at 6500m. From here on up hard snow and ice may be encountered. Continue over the Cresta del Viento and then on a path across the top of the Gran Accareo past a prominent vertical rock to the foot of the Canaleta. This is an appalling and unstable boulder slope which leads to the summit ridge at 6900m. Turn E and follow the ridge to reach the summit.

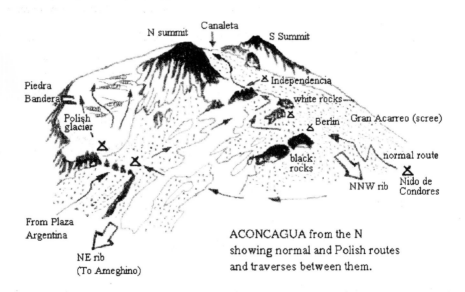

ACONCAGUA from the N
showing normal and Polish routes
and traverses between them.

**POLISH GLACIER ROUTE   PD**   Two or three higher camps are usually made. From Plaza Argentina base follow a path across moraines and penitentes. The first good camp is at c.4900m at the top of a steep slope, 1d. This has running water in the afternoons only. From here the route follows scree to gain the NE rib just L of the Ameghino col. Poor camp sites here at about 5600m. Follow the general line of the rib up towards the glacier, passing through or to the right of the rock teeth (several routes possible) to reach the high camps at the foot of Polish Glacier, 1d (several possibilities at 5700-5900m).

The Polish glacier is usually climbed in one day from here by the LHS passing close to the prominent banded rock face. This is called Piedra Bandera (6400m) because it looks like the

Argentine flag (campsites possible here). The glacier reaches about 40° just R of Piedra Bandera. A variation weaves its way up the centre (45°) and a harder (50°) variation takes the RHS. All finish by the E ridge - false summits. Descent is often made by the normal route. To gain the normal route from the Polish glacier high camp or vice versa several traverses or rising traverses are possible across scree and snow (all F).

**OTHER ROUTES**  The Ibañez - Marmillod route makes a rising traverse of the SW face from Plaza de Mulas to gain the SW ridge by a huge 45° couloir. The E glacier route starts from 4900m above Plaza Argentina on the Polish route.  There is a 60° section between the middle and upper glaciers. The route then climbs a 200m rock wall (to VI) then mixed ground to gain the E ridge at the top of the Polish glacier.

The huge 3000m S face has seen many different lines and variations climbed. Approach up the E side of the Lower Horcones valley from Confluencia  to Plaza Francia at 4500m (this is worth the walk for a look at this impressive face). The French Route climbs the central buttress direct to the N summit (VI, 55°). The even more desperate Slovene route takes a direct line to the S summit (VI, 90°, A3). See Secor's guide for a complete description of these and other routes.

**OTHER PEAKS**     From Plaza de Mulas the snow and ice peak **Cuerno 5462m, PD/AD** makes a good long training day.

**BEST MAP**   1:50,000 sketch map pub. 1987 American Alpine Club.

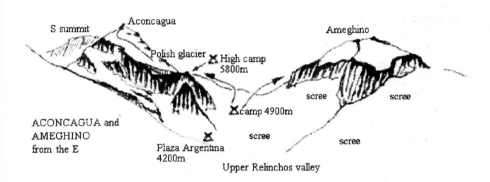

ACONCAGUA and AMEGHINO from the E

# Co. MIRADOR 6089m          Map 50                    6 days  N/K

This peak lies S of Aconcagua and provides superb views of the S face. Mirador is Spanish for viewpoint.

**ACCESS**  As for Aconcagua by the Horcones  valley to the foot of Q. Sargento Mas.

**CLIMB**  Climbed by the Q. Sargento Mas and the NW slopes. Grade n/k but not too difficult.

**BEST MAP**   As Aconcagua.

## Co. AMEGHINO  5883m          Map 50          10 days  PD/AD

Dwarfed by Aconcagua, Ameghino is nevertheless an impressive summit, with dramatic icefalls on the S face clearly seen from the Plaza Argentina base camp on Aconcagua. Frequently reported to be 6000m high with the height of 5883m possibly being for the E summit.

**ACCESS**  As for Aconcagua by the Vacas valley to Plaza Argentina base camp (4200m) and then the 4900m high camp.

**CLIMB**  From the 4900m camp Ameghino can be done in one long day. Climb easily to the col at 5380m and then up the SW ridge. Follow this mostly easy, but with one short section of about III, to the summit.

**BEST MAP**  As Aconcagua.

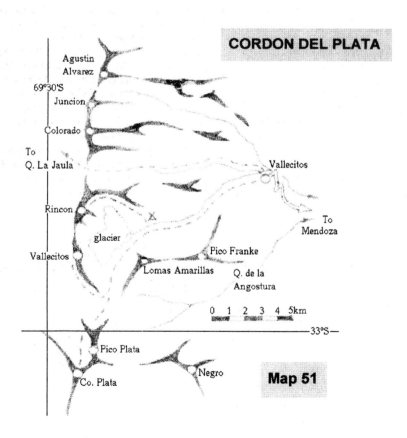

CORDON DEL PLATA

Agustin
Alvarez
69°30'S
Juncion
Colorado
To
Q. La Jaula
Rincon
glacier
Vallecitos
Vallecitos
To
Mendoza
Pico Franke
Lomas Amarillas
Q. de la
Angostura
0  1  2  3  4  5km
33°S
Pico Plata
Negro
Co. Plata

Map 51

**Co. PLATA** 5800m      Map 51      4 days      F
**Co. VALLECITOS** 5770m   Map 51      3 days  N/K
**Co. RINCON** 5500m      Map 51      3 days      F

These three peaks are in the range known as the Cordon del Plata and lie S of the Mendoza -
Santiago road only 50km from Mendoza. The range is very quiet compared to Aconcagua though
local Mendoza climbers are quite a common sight. There are a few small glaciers but most peaks
are rock scrambles. The names are of Spanish origin. Plata means silver, Vallecitos means 'small
valleys' and Rincon means corner.

**ACCESS** From Mendoza drive via the Potrerillos Hotel to the ski resort of Vallecitos (3100m).
No facilities in summer. From here walk up the Vallecitos valley SW over pleasant alpine
pastures then moraines to reach a high camp near the tongue of the Vallecitos glacier at about
4000m. Other sites, higher and lower, are possible

**PLATA CLIMB** From the camp below the Vallecitos glacier climb to the LHS of the glacier
to gain the bowl between Lomas Amarillas and Co. Vallecitos known as La Ollada (4500m).
Possible high camps here. Continue over easy ground S and SW to the summit.

**VALLECITOS CLIMB** An easy scramble grade probably about PD. Follow El Plata climb to
La Ollada then climb slopes W to reach the S ridge of Co. Vallecitos. Follow this to the summit.

**RINCON CLIMB** From the 4000m camp go up moraines around the S side of a brown peak
(point 4520m). Climb easily northwards on to the ridge (4500m) and follow this W to a snow
bowl (4800m). Climb the easy snow couloir on RHS of headwall then walk S to summit.

**OTHER ROUTES** The 'Supercanaleta' on Rincon is the obvious ice couloir splitting the E face.
Many harder routes have also been climbed on the E face of Co. Vallecitos.

**OTHER PEAKS Pico Franke 5100m,** can be climbed easily by the N ridge. **Lomas Amarillas
5300m,** can be climbed by easy E ridge from Pico Franke or by the harder SW ridge from the col
above La Ollada. For a harder challenge the mixed peak of Colorado is about IV and 60°.

**BEST MAP** No good maps. Use the one here or the poor AIGM 1:100,000 sheet.

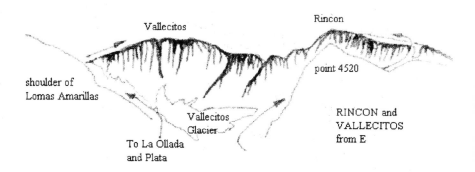

# SANTIAGO The capital of Chile                                       543m

Santiago the capital of Chile is a bustling city which lies at the foot of the Andes. On clear days (most common in spring and summer) it is possible to see the great humpbacked ice cap of Co. del Plomo 5424m, from the city centre. Access to the mountains around Co. del Plomo and the Maipu valley is very easy but the low altitude of Santiago can lead to acclimatisation problems.
The city is built along an E-W axis road, known as the Alameda (or O'Higgins) under which runs the main metro line. The smart suburbs and shopping areas are nearest the mountains and the poorest areas in the W near Estacion Central.
**FOOD** There are plenty of big supermarkets in Santiago selling a good range of food. Near the centre of town try those down San Diego, or near Estacion Central.
**FUEL** Most petrol stations sell kerosene. Camping Gas is available in most camping shops round town - try the Yellow Pages for the nearest one.
**SIGHTS** There is some nice architecture around the older part of town near the Presidential Palace. Near the centre of the old town **Co. Sta. Lucia 634m,** makes a worthy ascent for a view of the city and surrounding mountains, ½h. The hill is a maze of pathways and bizarre architecture that is a delight to explore on your first day of 35ºC, January weather! **Co. San Cristobal 880m,** with its funicular, gondola and huge statue of the virgin is another pleasant escape from the city fumes.
**MOUNTAIN TRANSPORT AND INFO** Try Southern Summits at Merced 102.
**MOUNTAIN EQUIPMENT** Try Southern Summits as above. There are several reasonable climbing and camping shops in the shopping centres up in Providencia. Try the one in Edif. Nueva Lyon #2189. There's also a camping shop at Merced 372.


# Co. JUNCAL 6110m          Map 52          6 days  N/K
# No. EL PLOMO 6070m        Map 52          8 days    F

Juncal is the peak which separates the Glaciar Juncal Sur (flowing into the Rio Olivares) from the Glaciar Juncal Norte (flowing N towards Portillo). El Plomo is the high border peak about 5km S of Juncal, and confusingly marked on ChIGM map as Co. Juncal. To add to the problems there is a Co. del Plomo 5424m, nearer to Santiago. In Spanish juncal is a reed bed and plomo is lead or lead coloured.
**ACCESS** From just below the bends on the main Mendoza - Santiago road at Portillo (PT) walk SE up the Rio Juncal. Take the RH valley at about 2800m to gain Glaciar Juncal Norte and follow this to a high camp beneath NW slopes of the peak.
**JUNCAL CLIMB** The normal route is by the NW glacier. Grade n/k but not difficult. Can also been climbed from Argentina.
**EL PLOMO** There are Inca ruins near the summit. Plomo is climbed easily by the Chilean side from the Olivares valley (4-5 day walk from Colorado valley - see Tupungato for access). The normal route on the mountain is a walk up the W slopes.
From the Argentine side by the N or NE ridge, technically difficult - approached via Rio de los Taguas.
**BEST MAP** ChIGM sheet 3300-7000 'Cord. de los Piuquenes' 1:50,000.

# Co. DEL PLOMO  5424m          Map 52          4 days     F

Not to be confused with No. El Plomo 6070m, which lies on the border about 20km to the NE. This is the peak seen prominently from Santiago as a curving ice-cap. It makes a fine acclimatisation ascent with easy access. Climbed by the Incas. A mummy was found buried near the summit in 1954, the first such discovery. This body proved that warts existed in the New World before Columbus arrived!

**ACCESS**    Drive from Santiago to the Valle Nevado ski resort (no facilities in summer). From here follow tracks to the hill at the top of the 4 person chair (3322m) or traverse slightly R of this to reach the Estero las Bayas valley behind. Climb up the far side of this valley keeping W of Co. Tres Puntas then descend Estero Las Yaretas to reach the main valley of the Estero Cepo. Follow this upstream past a camp by the large boulder at Piedra Numerada (3400m) to the base of the SW glaciers. Various camps here at 4000-4200m. 1½d from Valle Nevado. The Estero Cepo can also be reached from the La Parva ski centre but this is longer and involves more ascent.

**CLIMB**    From a high camp at the foot of the glaciers climb the RH and broader of two ribs on rock and scree (or the snowfield immediately L of this). Move L at top and go back over less steep ground to summit.

**OTHER PEAKS**    About 5km N of del Plomo is **Co. Altar 5180m, F** which can be climbed by its W ridge in 4 days from a road end at Villa Paulina (turn L before the bends up to La Parva and Valle Nevado).

**BEST MAP**    ChIGM sheet 3300-7000 'Cord. de los Piuquenes' 1:50,000. Sheet 3315-7000 'Rio Olivares' for access.

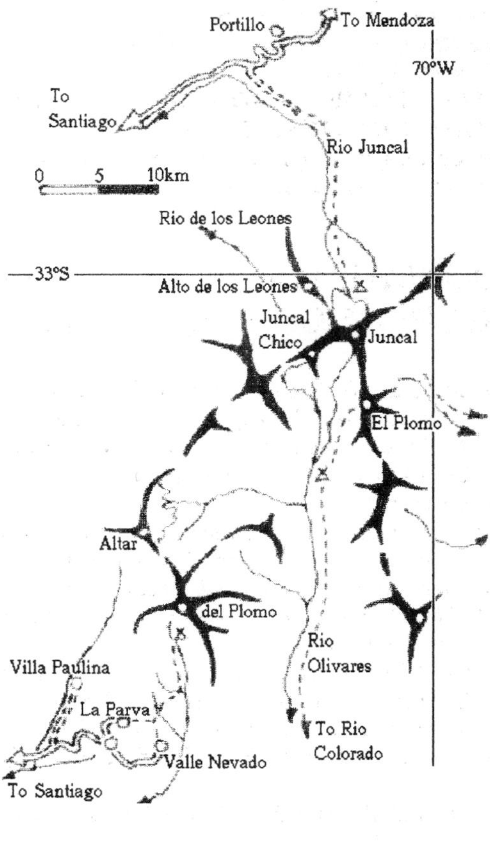

JUNCAL AREA

Map 52

To Mendoza
Portillo
70°W
To Santiago
Rio Juncal
0    5    10km
Rio de los Leones
33°S
Alto de los Leones
Juncal Chico
Juncal
El Plomo
Altar
del Plomo
Rio Olivares
Villa Paulina
La Parva
To Rio Colorado
Valle Nevado
To Santiago

## Co. DE LAS POLLERAS 5993m    Map 53                    8 days  N/K

Polleras is another high peak in the area and is one of the highest peak in the Andes not to reach 6000m! It lies on the border NW of Tupungato. In Spanish a pollera is a chicken run!

**ACCESS**  A base camp at c.4200m below the SW face of the mountain in the Estero de Morado can be reached in 2-3 days from Punta de Vacas by the Rio Tupungato and Rio del Plomo. Big river crossings. The Morado valley can probably also be gained from the Colorado river valley in Chile through the Portezuelo del Morado.

**CLIMB**  Polleras is usually climbed by the glacier on the W-SW slopes from the upper reaches of the Estero del Morado in Argentina. Grade probably about PD. 2d.

**BEST MAP**   ChIGM sheet 3300-6900 'San Jose de Maipo' 1:250,000

to summit

TUPUNGATO
summit block from N ridge

DEL PLOMO
SW face from
Piedra Numerada

summit lies behind

normal route

## Co. TUPUNGATO 6570m    Map 53              10 days   F

Tupungato is one of the highest peaks in the Andes and the third of the big peaks in the Santiago - Mendoza area, though Argentine surveys putting the mountain at 6800m are almost certainly erroneous. It is much quieter than Aconcagua but a very similar climb. Access is currently much shorter and easier from the Chilean side.

**ACCESS**  Long! From Santiago drive as far as possible up the Colorado river valley. A vehicle track goes to about where the Estero Parrraguirre comes in from N. Permission is needed from the ChilGener electricity company even if walking. From the end of the road walk along the S side of valley to a high camp at about 5000m  on the NW flanks of the mountain.  Some serious river crossings, 3-4d.

**CLIMB**   An easy ascent by the very broad N ridge. The route is open to a little variation and not complicated but involves a steep snow gully on the LHS to gain the summit block.

**OTHER ROUTES**  The N ridge of Tupungato can also be reached from Punta de Vacas or from the village of Tupungato in Argentina. Both routes involve 3-4 days walking and very serious river crossings (use mules). The S glacier is reported to be straightforward, the E glacier gives more difficult alpine routes.

**OTHER PEAKS**  To the S lies  **Tupungatito 5682m,** an active volcano and an easy ascent  by the N slopes from the Chilean side (upper Rio Colorado).

**BEST MAP**  ChIGM sheet 3300-6900 'San Jose de Maipo' 1:250,000

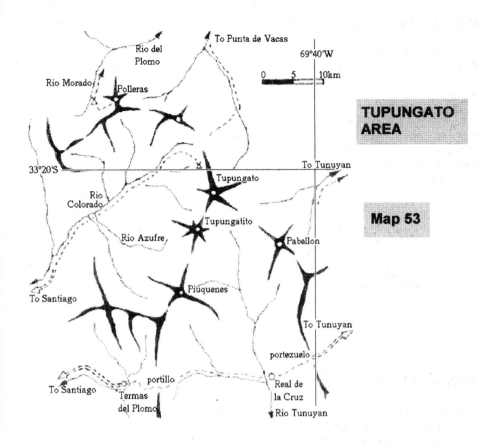

# Co. PABELLON 6152m       Map 53       8 days N/K
# No. DE LOS PIUQUENES 6019m  Map 53   8 days N/K

These two rarely visited peaks are outliers of the Tupungato massif. Piuquenes is on the border and Pabellon lies entirely within Argentina. Pabellon is also known as Co. Negro, Piuquenes is also known as Meson San Juan. Pabellon is a pavilion in Spanish.

**ACCESS** There is little information but the best routes appear to be as follows. For Pabellon follow the Rio de las Tunas from the village of Tunuyan in Argentina to get to the NE slopes of the mountain. For Piuquenes approach along the road from Tunuyan in Argentina to the Portezuelo Argentino then descend to the Rio Tunuyan and the refugio Real de la Cruz which lies SE of the peak (3000m) (facilities n/k) or approach on foot from the Rio Yeso in Chile through the Portillo de los Piuquenes (4080m) to reach the same refugio. River crossings will be serious.

**PIUQUENES CLIMB**   No definite details but the easiest route appears to be the S or E glaciers of this large flattish peak. Grade n/k but not desperate.

**PABELLON CLIMB**   Pabellon can be climbed from the NE but can also be climbed from the Refugio Real de la Cruz by the Rio Negro valley. No details of difficulty, but not thought to be hard.

**BEST MAP**   ChIGM sheet 3300-6900 'San Jose de Maipo' 1:250,000

## Co. MARMOLEJO 6108m     Map 54               6 days    F
## V. SAN JOSE  5856m             Map 54               5 days    F

Marmolejo is the southernmost 6000m peak in the Andes and, indeed, in the world. It has impressive faces on many sides but the W ridge provides an easy route to the summit. San Jose is an active volcano. The two peaks can easily be combined in one expedition with a base camp at La Engorda. Marmolejo is named after a Chilean general.

**ACCESS**   From Santiago to the village of Baños Morales (PT) (1900m). There are a few basic shops, cafes and accommodation in this small mountain resort . Buses are very busy in summer. From Baños Morales follow the track up the main valley for about 5km and cross river, then follow the path N around a ridge into the flat grassy area known as La Engorda (2600m). For San Jose climb up the Q. La Engorda (first SE then NE) to a refuge at 3500m on the ridge on the LHS (condition n/k). For Marmolejo follow the Estero Colina N for about 10km (several crossings may be necessary) to reach the head of the valley. Climb the slightly higher RHS of col by steep snow slopes to reach point 4138m (erroneously marked 138 on ChIGM). There is good camping on the N side of the ridge here.

An alternative approach for Marmolejo is from the Rio Yeso to the N. A bad 4WD road from San Gabriel up the Rio Yeso to Termas del Plomo. Make a serious river crossing here then an easy walk S up the Estero del Plomo valley to point 4138.

**MARMOLEJO CLIMB**   From the col at 4138m follow the broad plateau like W ridge sometimes on scree and rock sometimes on glacier (few crevasses) to reach the easy final summit cone of screes. A higher camp will probably be necessary near the glacier.

**SAN JOSE CLIMB**   Climb easily from the refuge NE to the crater rim, mostly on scree but with some snow.

**BEST MAP**   For Marmolejo ChIGM sheet 3330-6945 'Rio Yeso' 1:50,000. For San Jose ChIGM sheet 3345-6945 'Volcan San Jose' 1:50,000.

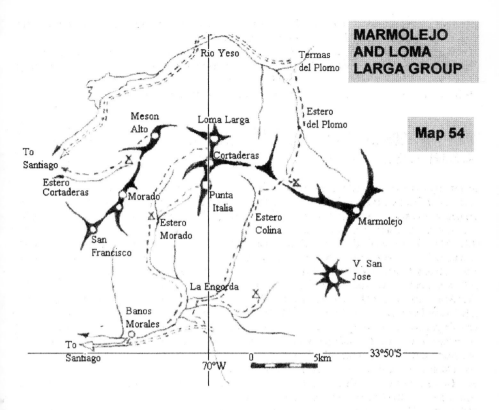

**MARMOLEJO AND LOMA LARGA GROUP**

**Map 54**

| | | | |
|---|---|---|---|
| **LOMA LARGA** | 5425m | Map 54 | 4 days  PD |
| **MESÓN ALTO** | 5297m | Map 54 | 4 days  PD |

These peaks are the two highest points of a compact group of peaks which give some of the best and most accessible 'alpine' climbing in this part of the Andes. They lie immediately W of Marmolejo. From a high base camp at about 4000m in the Morado valley a number of good days out can be enjoyed. The Estero Cortaderas to the W of group should not be confused with the peak known as Cortaderas in the E. Loma Larga is Spanish for the big hill and Mesón Alto translates as the high table.

**ACCESS**  For the majority of the routes go from Santiago to the village of Baños Morales (see above). From Baños Morales (1900m) follow a path on the N side of the main valley E then go N up the Estero Morado to a base camp on the glacier moraines at about 4000m. 1-2d.

Other routes can be reached from the Rio Yeso valley. From Santiago drive towards Baños Morales but turn off the road (to the N) just after San Gabriel and follow the track up the Rio Yeso to km17.

**LOMA LARGA CLIMBS**  The Loma Larga is an E-W ridge with 3 summits of nearly equal height, but with the highest at the W end. This summit is climbed easily (PD) by the S glacier.

For the Central summit (PD/AD) climb the same glacier but turn towards the Loma Larga - Cortaderas col then follow the S ridge. Similarly to reach the E peak (AD).

**MESON ALTO CLIMB**   Meson Alto is a N-S ridge of 3 peaks, the N being the highest. The normal route is from the Rio Yeso valley to the W. From km17 (2100m) climb the Estero Cortaderas to the base of the glacier at over 4000m. Climb the glacier turning seracs to a camp at the base of the SW peak. Cross the glacier to the N and climb up to the L of the N summit by a couloir (PD). There are very difficult routes on the S face from the Morado valley (TD, 60°, IV)

**OTHER PEAKS**   From a high camp in the Morado valley many other climbs can be done besides Loma Larga. These include **Cortaderas 5220m, PD** climbed from the Cortaderas - Loma Larga col (see above) by the rocky N ridge. **Punta Italia 4978m, AD** is normally climbed from the W from a camp at the tongue of the glacier. Climb by the RHS of glacier to gain an easy couloir which leads to the Punta Italia - Cortaderas ridge. From here climb to summit by the N ridge (III). The N summit of **Morado 5060m, PD** is the highest. It is also normally climbed from the Morado valley by the SE glacier. From a camp in the valley climb an easy rock wall to reach a high camp by the glacier at 4500m. From this camp cross the glacier to the N and climb the final cone by any of a variety of routes.

From a camp in the Estero Cortaderas (see under Meson Alto above) **San Francisco 4940m, F** can be climbed by the N slopes without difficulty. The 1400m S face has seen a number of difficult routes.

**BEST MAP**   ChIGM sheet 3330-7000 'Embalse El Yeso' 1:50,000.

# THE 6000m PEAKS OF THE ANDES IN ORDER OF HEIGHT

All heights are in metres.

The criterion used to select this list is a re-ascent height of 400m from any higher peak. This figure was chosen for several reasons: any larger re-ascent eliminates some of the most notable summits such as Tocllaraju, Jirishanca and Illampu. Any lesser re-ascent criterion includes many minor summits such as the N and E peaks of Coropuna. By this criterion there are also a rather elegant ninety nine 6000m peaks in the Andes. 19 of these are in the Cordillera Blanca of Peru and 35 are in the Puna de Atacama.

In many areas of South America, particularly in Argentina, the heights of many peaks are subject to debate. Some peaks having quoted heights that differ by 300m or more. The heights given here are thought to be the most widely accepted figures, many are taken from the most recent Argentine survey.

The peaks are arranged in groups of ten. The grades given are for the easiest ascent route. An asterisk by the date of first ascent denotes a peak known to have had a Pre-Columbian ascent, or on which ruins have been found high up. The date of the first modern ascent is also given. Dates in brackets indicate a disputed first ascent.

| PEAK | HEIGHT | | AREA | COUNTRY | 1st ASCENT |
|------|--------|------|------|---------|------------|
| Aconcagua | 6959 | F | High Andes | Argentina | 1897* |
| Pissis | 6882 | F | Puna | Argentina | 1937 |
| Ojos del Salado | 6864 | F/PD | Puna | Argentina-Chile | 1937 |
| Mercedario | 6770 | F | High Andes | Argentina | 1934* |
| Huascarán Sur | 6768 | PD | Cord. Blanca | Peru | 1932 |
| Bonete | 6759 | F | Puna | Argentina | 1954 |
| Tres Cruces Sur | 6749 | F | Puna | Argentina-Chile | 1937 |
| Llullaillaco | 6739 | F | Northern Puna | Argentina-Chile | 1952* |
| Cazadero | 6658 | F | Puna | Argentina | 1970 |
| Huascarán Norte | 6655 | PD | Cord. Blanca | Peru | (1908) |
| | | | | | |
| Yerupajá | 6634 | D | Cord. Huayhuash | Peru | 1950 |
| Tres Cruces Cent. | 6629 | F | Puna | Chile | 1973 |
| Incahuasi | 6621 | F | Puna | Argentina-Chile | 1913* |
| Tupungato | 6570 | F | High Andes | Argentina-Chile | 1897 |
| Sajama | 6542 | PD | Cord. Occidental | Bolivia | 1939 |
| Nacimiento | 6490 | F | Puna | Argentina | 1937 |
| El Muerto | 6476 | F | Puna | Chile | 1950 |
| Illimani | 6462 | PD+ | Cord. Real | Bolivia | 1898 |
| Antofalla | 6440 | F | Puna | Argentina | 1954* |
| Veladero | 6436 | F | Puna | Argentina | n/k |

| PEAK | HEIGHT | | AREA | COUNTRY | 1st ASCENT |
|---|---|---|---|---|---|
| Ancohuma | 6427 | PD+ | Cord. Real | Bolivia | 1919 |
| Coropuna | 6425 | F | Cord. Occidental | Peru | 1911* |
| Ramada | 6410 | n/k | High Andes | Argentina | 1934 |
| Huantsan | 6395 | TD | Cord. Blanca | Peru | 1952 |
| Huandoy | 6395 | AD/D | Cord. Blanca | Peru | 1932 |
| Ausangate | 6384 | PD+ | Cord. Vilcanota | Peru | 1953 |
| del Toro | 6380 | F | High Andes | Argentina-Chile | 1964* |
| Libertador | 6380 | F | Northern Puna | Argentina | 1950 |
| Illampu | 6368 | AD+ | Cord. Real | Bolivia | 1928 |
| Chopicalqui | 6356 | AD | Cord. Blanca | Peru | 1932 |
| Siula Grande | 6352 | D | Cord. Huayhuash | Peru | 1936 |
| Parinacota | 6342 | F | Cord. Occidental | Chile - Bolivia | 1928 |
| Tortolas | 6332 | F | High Andes | Argentina - Chile | 1924* |
| Reclus | 6320 | F | Puna | Argentina | n/k* |
| Chimborazo | 6310 | F | Ecuador | Ecuador | 1880 |
| Ampato | 6288 | F | Cord. Occidental | Peru | 1966* |
| Palcaraju | 6274 | n/k | Cord. Blanca | Peru | 1939 |
| Salkantay | 6271 | AD | Cord. Vilcabamba | Peru | 1952 |
| Santa Cruz | 6259 | D+ | Cord. Blanca | Peru | 1948 |
| Olivares | 6252 | n/k | High Andes | Argentina-Chile | 1964 |
| Belgrano | 6250 | F | Puna | Argentina | 1947 |
| Tres Quebradas | 6250 | F | Puna | Argentina-Chile | 1937 |
| Pular | 6225 | F | Northern Puna | Chile | 1960* |
| Chinchey | 6222 | AD | Cord. Blanca | Peru | 1939 |
| Pomerape | 6222 | F | Cord. Occidental | Chile - Bolivia | (1946) |
| Solo | 6190 | F | Puna | Argentina-Chile | (1949) |
| Copa | 6188 | PD+ | Cord. Blanca | Peru | 1932 |
| El Ermitaño | 6187 | F | Puna | Chile | 1967 |
| Aucanquilcha | 6176 | F | Cord. Occidental | Chile | 1935* |
| Ranrapalca | 6162 | D | Cord. Blanca | Peru | 1939 |
| Los Gemelos | 6159 | F | Puna | Argentina | n/k |
| San Pedro | 6154 | F | Cord. Occidental | Chile | 1903 |
| Pabellón | 6152 | n/k | High Andes | Argentina | 1969 |
| Pucaranra | 6147 | AD+ | Cord. Blanca | Peru | 1948 |
| Queva | 6135 | F | Northern Puna | Argentina | n/k* |
| Sierra Nevada | 6127 | n/k | Puna | Argentina-Chile | n/k |
| Hualcan | 6125 | n/k | Cord. Blanca | Peru | 1939 |
| Barrancas Blancas | 6119 | F | Puna | Chile | n/k |
| San Pablo | 6118 | F | Cord. Occidental | Chile | 1910 |
| Chacraraju | 6113 | ED | Cord. Blanca | Peru | 1956 |

| PEAK | HEIGHT | | AREA | COUNTRY | 1st ASCENT |
|------|--------|---|------|---------|-----------|
| Juncal | 6110 | n/k | High Andes | Argentina-Chile | 1911 |
| Callangate | 6110 | n/k | Cord. Vilcanota | Peru | 1957 |
| Marmolejo | 6108 | F | High Andes | Argentina-Chile | 1928 |
| El Condor | 6108 | n/k | Puna | Argentina | n/k |
| Jatunriti | 6106 | n/k | Cord. Vilcanota | Peru | 1955 |
| Chearoco | 6104 | AD | Cord. Real | Bolivia | 1928 |
| Huayna Potosi | 6094 | PD | Cord. Real | Bolivia | 1919 |
| Jirishanca | 6094 | D/TD | Cord. Huayhuash | Peru | 1957 |
| Solimana | 6093 | n/k | Cord. Occidental | Peru | 1970 |
| Jatunhuma | 6093 | n/k | Cord. Vilcanota | Peru | 1957 |
| | | | | | |
| Mirador | 6089 | n/k | High Andes | Argentina | 1953 |
| Chachani | 6084 | F | Cord. Occidental | Peru | 1889* |
| Aracar | 6080 | F | Northern Puna | Argentina | 1958* |
| Colorados | 6080 | n/k | Puna | Argentina-Chile | n/k |
| Copiapó | 6080 | F | Puna | Chile | 1937* |
| El Plomo | 6070 | F | High Andes | Argentina-Chile | 1910 |
| Pumasillo | 6070 | n/k | Cord. Vilcabamba | Peru | 1957 |
| Vicuñas | 6067 | n/k | Puna | Chile | n/k |
| Guallatiri | 6063 | F | Cord. Occidental | Chile | 1926 |
| Chañi | 6060 | F | Northern Puna | Argentina | 1901* |
| | | | | | |
| El Fraile | 6060 | n/k | Puna | Argentina-Chile | n/k |
| Acotango | 6050 | n/k | Cord. Occidental | Chile - Bolivia | 1965 |
| Yayamari | 6049 | n/k | Cord. Vilcanota | Peru | 1957 |
| Pucajirca | 6046 | n/k | Cord. Blanca | Peru | 1961 |
| Pili | 6046 | F | Northern Puna | Chile | 1939* |
| Chaupi Orco | 6044 | PD | Cord. Apolobamba | Bolivia - Peru | 1958 |
| Quitaraju | 6040 | AD | Cord. Blanca | Peru | 1936 |
| Contrahierbas | 6036 | n/k | Cord. Blanca | Peru | 1939 |
| Tocllaraju | 6032 | AD/D | Cord. Blanca | Peru | 1939 |
| Socompa | 6031 | F | Northern Puna | Argentina-Chile | 1905* |
| | | | | | |
| Peña Blanca | 6030 | F | Puna | Chile | 1956* |
| Salin | 6029 | n/k | Northern Puna | Argentina-Chile | 1960* |
| Hualca Hualca | 6025 | n/k | Cord. Occidental | Peru | n/k |
| Artesonraju | 6025 | AD/D | Cord. Blanca | Peru | 1932 |
| Caraz | 6025 | PD | Cord. Blanca | Peru | 1955 |
| Palpana | 6022 | F | Cord. Occidental | Chile | 1977* |
| San Francisco | 6020 | F | Puna | Argentina-Chile | 1913 |
| Piuquenes | 6019 | n/k | High Andes | Argentina-Chile | 1933 |
| Uturunco | 6009 | F | Cord. Lipez | Bolivia | 1955 |

The peaks of Palermo and Quemado in the Argentine Puna near Salta and the peak of Vallecitos near Colorados, may qualify. It is not known whether they have sufficient re-ascent height to class as independent peaks.

The following peaks, all sometimes quoted higher than 6000m have been omitted from the list because there is considerable doubt as to whether they are over 6000m. Chachacomani 5998m, Lasunayoc 5960m, Nuevo Mundo 5929m, Laguna Blanca 5900m, Galan 5912m, Pilar de los Pailas 5900m, Plata 5800m, Ameghino 5883m.

The peak which is not 6000m but makes the top 100 is:

Chachacomani    5998    PD    Cord. Real    Bolivia    1947

For interest the 10 peaks which just miss the top 100 are the following:

| Polleras | 5993 | n/k | High Andes | Chile-Argentina | 1908 |
| Mojones | 5990 | n/k | Puna | Argentina | n/k |
| Capurata | 5990 | n/k | Cord. Occidental | Chile-Bolivia | 1967 |
| Alto Toroni | 5990 | n/k | Cord. Occidental | Chile-Bolivia | n/k |
| Tacora | 5988 | n/k | Cord. Occidental | Chile | 1904 |
| Ansilta | 5984 | n/k | High Andes | Argentina | 1950's |
| Sairecabur | 5971 | F | Cord. Occidental | Chile-Bolivia | 1980 |
| Peladito | 5970 | n/k | Puna | Argentina | n/k |
| Lasunayoc | 5960 | n/k | Cord. Vilcabamba | Peru | 1956 |
| Paniri | 5960 | F | Cord. Occidental | Chile | 1980* |

Other famous peaks and their approximate positions are Alpamayo (116th), Cotopaxi (130th), Misti (154th). There are about170 peaks over 5800m and somewhere over 400 peaks of 5000m or more with a re-ascent of more than 400m. We'll publish a full list one day!

# A BRIEF MOUNTAINEERING HISTORY OF THE HIGH ANDES

| | |
|---|---|
| 1400-1500's | Repeated ascents of many peaks by native Indians at the time of the Inca Empire including Llullaillaco 6739m, Licancabur 5916m, del Toro 6380m, Queva 6135m and almost certainly Aconcagua 6960m. |
| 1736 | Chimborazo surveyed at 6310m and believed to be the world's highest mountain for the next 70 years. An early attempt to climb the peak fails. |
| 1802 | Humboldt reaches 5800m on Chimborazo. |
| 1872 | Reid and Escobar ascend Cotopaxi 5897m. |
| 1880 | Whymper, with the Carrels as guides ascends Chimborazo 6310m, Antisana and Cayambe in Ecuador. |
| 1897 | The Swiss guide Zurbriggen ascends Aconcagua 6960m alone. Vines and Zurbriggen also make the first ascent of Tupungato 6570m. |
| 1898 | Conway makes the first ascent of Illimani 6462m in Bolivia. |
| 1908 | Disputed first ascent of Huascaran North 6654m, by Annie Peck, an American schoolmistress. |
| 1930's | German and Austrian expeditions under E Schneider ascend many peaks in the Peruvian Cordilleras Blanca and Huayhuash, including Huascaran Sur, Huandoy and Chopicalqui in 1932 and Siula Grande in 1936. |
| 1937 | Polish expedition makes first ascent of Ojos del Salado 6885m, Pissis 6779m and many other 6000m Puna peaks. |
| 1939 | First ascents of Colombia's two highest peaks, Colon and Bolivar by American and German expeditions. |
| 1950's | Extensive exploration and many first ascents in the Peruvian Andes including Yerupaja in 1950 (American), Salkantay in 1952 (Anglo-French), Ausangate in 1953 (German) and Pumasillo in 1957 (British). |
| 1952 | Ruins, figurines, pottery etc. found near summit of Llullaillaco by the first modern ascensionists. |
| 1954 | A French expedition climbs the huge and dangerous south face of Aconcagua. |
| 1954 | A mummy is discovered on Co. del Plomo near Santiago, the first such discovery. |
| 1956 | A French expedition makes the first ascent of Chacraraju, the last and most difficult of the 6000m peaks in the Cordillera Blanca. |
| 1957 | First ascent of Alpamayo, by a German expedition. |
| 1963 | First ascent of Altar, Ecuador's most difficult peak. |
| 1966 | Paragot route climbed, the first on the huge 1500m N face of Huascaran Norte. |
| 1970's-1980's | The last remote 6000m peaks in the Puna de Atacama and Cordillera Occidental are climbed. |
| late 70's-80's | Climbers in the Cord. Blanca begin the exploration of the harder ice faces e.g. the S faces of Chacraraju and Ocshapalca and the W face of the needle Cayesh. |
| 1985 | Joe Simpson and Simon Yates climb the W face of Siula Grande, one of the last big unclimbed faces in the Andes. Joe breaks his leg on the way down.... |

# THE INCA MOUNTAINEERS

Perhaps the most fascinating aspect of the history of climbing in the Andes is the large number of ascents which were made around the time of the Inca Empire (c. 1400-1530). The highest peak they are known to have climbed is Llullaillaco 6739m on the Chile-Argentina border. A few metres below the summit are a couple of primitive huts, a sight which must have surprised the Polish expedition who thought they were making the first ascent in 1952. Archaeological expeditions have since unearthed pieces of cloth, pottery, wooden utensils and statuettes on this and many other peaks. The indications are that considerable periods of time were spent at the summits of many of the peaks in the Cordillera Occidental, Cordillera Lipez, Puna de Atacama and High Andes.

The first discoveries were made as long ago as 1884 on Licancabur but it was only in the 1950's and 1960's when the first mummified corpses were discovered (on the summits of del Plomo 5424m and del Toro 6380m) that interest in high altitude archaeology really began. Burial sites have now been found on many peaks of over 5500m. Unfortunately many of these have been disturbed by grave robbers.

Ascents seem to have been made mostly for religious purposes, though it is possible that the peaks were also used as watchtowers or signal stations. Mountains are still worshipped in many parts of the Andes. Though there are many reasons for this mountain worship the main reason appears to be as a source of water and fertility. Johan Rheinard states that peaks with crater lakes (such as Licancabur) appear to have been especially important.

There is now no doubt that one purpose of the ascents was to make sacrifices. Human victims have been found on many peaks including del Toro (neck wound), Pichu Pichu, Aconcagua (strangled) and most recently Ampato (sharp blow to skull). The bodies, which are nearly always of adolescents or young adults, are commonly referred to as mummies. Technically they are not mummies, because they have only been preserved accidentally by the very cold and dry conditions prevalent. Most remains have been dated to the time of the Inca Empire though the ascents were not necessarily all made by the Inca's themselves.

It now seems probable that the Incas or their subjects climbed Aconcagua. In 1947 a guanaco was discovered at over 6800m on the ridge connecting the N and S summits. More recently, in 1985 a grave containing a sacrifice victim was discovered lower on the mountain. Technically the summit is no more difficult than Llullaillaco. Due to the difficulties of investigation and the lack of written records from the time of the Incas (who had no written language) we may never know for sure.

For more information on this fascinating subject see the articles by Johan Reinhard in the National Geographic, March 1992 and American Alpine Journal 1983, or the article by Evelio Echevarria in the Alpine Journal no.73 (1968).

# SELECTED BIBLIOGRAPHY

OOP = Out of Print

MOUNTAINEERING TECHNIQUE
Glacier Travel and Crevasse Rescue, **Selter,** Diadem Books 1990
Handbook of Climbing, **Fyffe and Peter**, Pelham Books 1990
A Manual of Modern Rope Techniques, **Shepherd**, Constable 1990
NOLS Wilderness Mountaineering, **Powers**, Stackpole Books 1993

MOUNTAINEERING MEDICINE
Medicine for Mountaineering, **Wilkerson**, The Mountaineers 1992
Altitude Illness, **Bezruchka**, The Mountaineers 1994
Medical Handbook for Mountaineers, **Steele**, Constable 1988

ENGLISH LANGUAGE CLIMBING AND WALKING GUIDES
Guide to the Worlds Mountains (3rd Ed.) **Kelsey**, Kelsey Publishing 1990.
Mountaineering in the Andes, **Neate**, Expedition Advisory Centre, RGS 1994.
Bradt Publications - Trekking guides to Peru + Bolivia 1995, Chile + Argentina 1994. Climbing
      and Hiking guide to Ecuador 1994.
Climbs of the Cordillera Blanca, **Sharman**, Whizzo Climbs 1995
Yuraq Janka, **Ricker**, American Alpine Club 1977
The Peruvian Andes (Cordillera Blanca and Huayhuash), **Beaud**, Cordee 1988 (OOP)
Southern Cordillera Real, **Pecher and Schmiemann**, Plata 1977 (OOP)
Aconcagua, **Secor**, The Mountaineers 1994.

SPANISH LANGUAGE CLIMBING GUIDES
Ecuador - Montañas del Sol, **Serrano - Rojas - Landazuri**, Ediciones Campo Abierto 1994
Bolivia - Cordillerra Real, **Mesili,** Los Amigos del Libro 1984 (OOP)

GENERAL TRAVEL GUIDES
South American Handbook, Trade and Travel Publications. A detailed travel guide to the
      whole continent, revised annually.
Lonely Planet Publications - Good general guidebooks to the individual countries of South
      America, revised every few years.
Insight guides - General guidebooks to the individual countries, less informative but with good
      pictures!

MAPS
The best maps are usually those published by the national IGM's but these are only available in
South America (see page 11). Good maps normally available in Europe and the US include:
ITMB sheet 081 (Venezuela to Bolivia) ISBN 0 921463 08 1
ITMB sheet 155 (Chile and Argentina) ISBN 0 921463 16 2
ITMB sheet 278 (Ecuador) ISBN 0 921463 27 8
Alpenvereinskarte, Cordillera Real sheets 0/8 and 0/9

Alpenvereinskarte, Cordillera Blanca sheets 0/3a and 0/3b
Alpenvereinskarte, Cordillera Huayhuash sheet 0/3c

NATURAL HISTORY
South Americas National Parks, **Leitch**, The Mountaineers 1990.
The Flight of the Condor, **Andrews**, Collins 1982 (OOP)

ANDEAN HISTORY
Kingdom of the Sun God, **Cameron**, Facts on File 1990
Conquest of the Incas, **Hemming**, Macmillan 1970
Sacred Peaks of the Andes, **Reinhard,** National Geographic magazine 181, 1992 - an excellent
    article on Inca ascents.

CLASSIC MOUNTAINEERING LITERATURE
Touching the Void, **Simpson**,  Cape 1988 and paperback editions
The Puma's Claw, **Clark,** Hutchinson 1959 (OOP)
Travels amongst the Great Andes of the Equator, **Whymper**, John Murray 1891 or  Charles
    Knight 1972 (OOP)
Aconcagua - South Face, **Poulet and Ferlet**, Constable 1956 (OOP)
The Highest Andes, **FitzGerald**, Methuen 1899 (OOP)
The Butcher: The ascent of Yerupajá, **Sack**, 1952 (OOP)
The Andes are Prickly, **Slesser**, 1966 (OOP)
A search for the Apex of America, **Peck**, 1911 (OOP)

# ACKNOWLEDGEMENTS

This guide could not have been compiled without the help of many people. In particular the
following deserve special mention.

Damian Aurelio V., Huaraz, information
Derek Bearhop, Edinburgh, photographs and comments
Linda Biggar, Castle Douglas, support both on and off the mountains
Gordon Biggar, Edinburgh, proof reading and photographs
Bob Black, Bogota, information
Marcos Frischknecht, Bariloche, information
Gregory Horne, Jasper, Alberta, information and photographs
Alfredo Martinez D., La Paz, information
Matthew Shaw, Edinburgh, proof reading, photographs and information
Ivan Vigouroux, Santiago, information

# MOUNTAINEERS VOCABULARY

See also geographical glossary for more general terms such as ridge, buttress, etc.

| ENGLISH | SPANISH |
| --- | --- |
| above | arriba |
| abseil | rappel |
| altitude | altura |
| altitude sickness | soroche |
| anchor | ancla |
| ascent | subida |
| ash | ceniza |
| belay (point) | reunion |
| to belay | asegurar |
| below | abajo |
| bivouac | vivac |
| boots | botas |
| climb | escalada |
| (to) climb | escalar |
| crack | fisura, grieta |
| crampons | grampones |
| (to) cross | atravesar |
| degrees | grados |
| (to) descend | bajar |
| distant | lejos |
| donkey | burro |
| exposed | aereo, expuesto |
| frozen | congelado |
| (to) go down | bajar |
| (to) go up | subir |
| guide | guia |
| hammer | martillo |
| hanging | suspendido, colgante |
| ice | hielo |
| ice-axe | piolet |
| ice-screw | tornillo |
| karabiner | mosquetone |
| kerosene | kerosina |
| (to) leave | dejar |
| ledge | cornisa, terraza |
| left | izquierda |
| lightning | relampago |
| loose | suelto |
| map | mapa |
| mountaineer | andinista-alpinista |
| mule driver | arriero |
| near | cerca |
| normal route | via normal |
| nut | empotrador |
| overhang | desplome |
| paraffin | kerosina |
| path | sendero |
| petrol | gasolina |
| (to) pick up | recoger |
| pick-up truck | camioneta |
| pitch | largo |
| piton, peg | clavo |
| porter | porteador |
| rain | lluvia |
| right | derecha |
| rock | roca |
| roof | techo |
| rope | cuerda, soga |
| (to) rope up | encordar |
| route | via |
| rucksack | mochilla |
| sand | arena |
| slab | placa |
| snow | nieve |
| (to) snow | nevar |
| stance | reunion |
| steep | pendiente |
| storm | tormenta, tempuesto |
| stove | cocina, estufa |
| straight on | derecho |
| tent | carpa |
| traverse | travesia |
| (to) traverse | atravesar |
| truck | camion |
| (to) walk | caminar |
| white gas | bencina blanca |
| wind | viento |

# GEOGRAPHICAL GLOSSARY

All words are Spanish unless otherwise
indicated. Q = Quechua,  A = Aymará
The Spanish alphabet is used. The letter Ñ
follows N, the letter LL follows L.
Words relating more specifically to climbing
appear in the mountaineers vocabulary.

| SPANISH | ENGLISH |
|---|---|
| abra | pass |
| acequia | aqueduct |
| aguja | needle |
| altiplano | high altitude plateau of Peru and Bolivia |
| arista | ridge (arete) |
| arroyo | stream |
| baños | thermals |
| bofedal | bog, swamp |
| caida de hielo | icefall |
| camino | path |
| canaleta | gully |
| cara | face |
| carreterrra | road |
| casa | house |
| cascada | waterfall |
| cerro | hill, mountain |
| cocha, cota (Q, A) | lake |
| collado | col |
| contrafuerte | buttress |
| cordillera | mountain range |
| cresta | ridge |
| cueva | cave |
| cumbre | summit |
| espolon | spur, buttress |
| estancia | large farm (sometimes now a small village) |
| este | east |
| estero | stream |
| glaciar | glacier |
| grande | big |
| grieta | crevasse |
| hacienda | ranch |
| hierba | pasture |
| hito | cairn, marker |
| huanca (Q) | rock |
| janka, hanca (Q) | snow peak |
| jirka (Q) | mountain |
| lago, laguna | lake, lagoon |
| loma | hill |
| mina | mine |
| monte | mount |
| muro | wall |
| nevado | snow mountain |
| norte | north |
| occidental | western |
| oeste | west |
| oriental | eastern |
| pampa (Q) | meadow, plain, plateau |
| paramo | moorland, often wet |
| pared | wall |
| paso | pass |
| pata (Q) | summit, hill |
| penitentes | vertical spikes of snow from 10cm to 5m high |
| peña | large rock |
| piedra | rock |
| portachuelo | pass |
| portezuelo | pass |
| puca (Q) | red |
| puente | bridge |
| puna (Q) | high altitude plateau of Chile and Argentina |
| punta | point |
| quebrada | ravine-gorge-river |
| razo, raju  (Q) | snow summit |
| refugio | mountain hut |
| rio | river |
| riti (Q) | snow peak |
| salar | salt lake |
| salto | waterfall |
| sendero | path |
| sierra | mountain range |
| sur | south |
| talud | scree |
| termas | thermal springs |
| torre | tower |
| urcu, orco (Q) | mountain |
| valle | valley |
| yana (Q) | black |
| yurac (Q) | white |

## ABBREVIATIONS

| | |
|---|---|
| N/K or n/k | Not Known |
| Co., No. | Cerro, Nevado |
| Po., Sa. | Pico, Sierra |
| V. | Volcan |
| Lag. | Lago, Laguna |
| R. | Rio, River |
| Q. | Quebrada |
| Hac. | Hacienda |
| N, S, E, W | North, South, East and West. |
| 4WD | Four wheel drive |
| (PT) | last place reached by Public Transport |
| L, R, LH, RH LHS, RHS | Left, Right, Left-hand Left-Hand Side, etc. Refer to direction of travel unless stated otherwise. |
| d., h. | days, hours |
| BIGM, ChIGM etc. | National Instituto Geografico Militar - Equivalent to the Ordnance Survey as a source of maps |
| UIAGM | International Mountain Guides Assosciation |
| pub. | published |

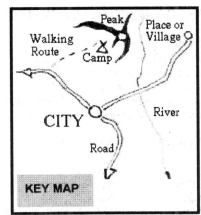

KEY MAP

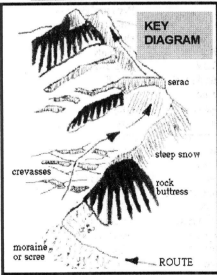

KEY DIAGRAM

serac

steep snow

crevasses

rock buttress

moraine or scree

ROUTE

KEY TITLE BAR

| | | | | |
|---|---|---|---|---|
| **SALKANTAY** | 6271m | Map 22 | 8 days | AD |
| **HUMANTAY** | 5917m | Map 22 | 7 days | AD+ |

MOUNTAIN NAME   Height            Best map in the text       Days to climb   Grade
(Large text = principal 6000m peak)                          this peak alone
(Small text = 5000m peak or subsidiary 6000m peak)

# GEOGRAPHICAL INDEX

All minor words such as del, el, los and all mountain descriptions such as Pico, Cerro etc. are ignored.
The Spanish alphabet is used. The letter Ñ follows N, the letter LL follows L  and CH follows C.

All entries are peaks unless stated.
Abbreviations used for other entries are -

Cord.   cordillera
T        town or city

Where there are two or more identical names the country is indicated as follows -

A    Argentina
B    Bolivia
Co   Colombia
Ch   Chile
E    Ecuador
P    Peru
V    Venezuela

# SUBJECT INDEX